CREATIVE BIBLE LEARNING

FOR ADULTS

BY BOBBIE REED

Regal Books

A Division of GL Publications
Ventura, California, U.S.A.

Published by Regal Books
A Division of GL Publications
Ventura, California 93006
Printed in U.S.A.

Library of Congress Catalog Card Number 77-76206
ISBN 0-8307-0480-9

5 6 7 8 9 10 / 91 90 89

Rights for publishing this book in other languages are contracted by Gospel Literature International (GLINT) foundation. GLINT also provides technical help for the adaptation, translation, and publishing of Bible study resources and books in scores of languages worldwide. For further information, contact GLINT, Post Office Box 488, Rosemead, California, 91770, U.S.A., or the publisher.

Contents

The Authors

Bobbie Reed attended Arizona Bible College. She has taught Sunday School, worked with Vacation Bible Schools and Bible clubs, and co-sponsored youth groups for 16 years in several churches across the United States.

Bobbie is currently Director of Staff Development for one of California's state agencies, and is completing her Master's degree in Public Administration at California State University at Los Angeles, teaching at Coastline Community College in Fountain Valley, California, and serving as Managing Editor for *SOLO*, a Christian magazine for single adults.

Bobbie has also written Junior High and Adult curriculum for Gospel Light Publications, written for *TEACH* magazine and co-authored books for ICL (*Bible Learning Activities—Youth*, *Your Sunday School Can Grow*, and *Creative Bible Learning for Adults*).

Foreword

Gospel Light Publications is committed to obeying Christ's command to "Go . . . make disciples . . . and teach" (Matt. 28:19,20, *TLB*). To fulfill this great commission, Gospel Light provides in-depth training resources for leaders ministering in churches of all sizes.

This book is designed for both the new teacher and those who are more experienced. Bobbie Reed concisely presents the needs and characteristics of adults. She will help you discover a variety of ways you can provide effective Bible learning. These insights into your learners, the learning process, and appropriate methods and materials will enable you to make the Bible come alive for your learners.

You can profit from reading this book alone or by reading and discussing it with a group of teachers. You will want to refer to this book many times for assistance in planning new methods and programs as well as improving what you are already doing.

We trust that this book will help you as you obey Christ's command, "Go . . . make disciples . . . and teach."

PART 1
TEACHING

Seventeen-year-old Charlie stormed up the stairs after an argument with his parents, mumbling to himself. "Don't know why I can't go on that ski weekend with my friends. I'm old enough! I'm an adult!" ▪ Is he? ▪ Whether Charlie is considered an adult or not depends on who is judging him and with what criteria. He can get a driver's license. He can't vote or marry in most states without parental consent. But he may be tried as an adult if he were to commit a felony. ▪ What is an adult? How would you describe adulthood? Is adulthood indicated by the development of sexual maturity? Does a person become an adult when he reaches a certain age? Or is it a matter of entering an occupation or being eligible for military service? Some educators and psychologists place adulthood at 21, others at 24 and some at 18. ▪ No single criterion is

ADULTS

sufficient to define adulthood. ■ Once a person has completed or left high school and has passed his eighteenth birthday, he is usually considered an adult. And society expects him to begin to function in the manner prescribed for adulthood. We expect an adult to use his time constructively—get a job or go to college. We expect an adult to become mature, to achieve a balance in his life between work and play, to be in control of his life and assume responsibility for his behavior. ■ A teacher of adults needs to understand adults and how they learn in order to be effective in communicating the love of God to his class members. Part One of this book discusses the unique characteristics of adults at various age levels and the basic elements of adult learning.

Why Have an Adult Sunday School?

Jim and Sandy Taylor sat in their adult Sunday School classroom with their Bibles on their laps. Across from them sat Paul and Vicki Hamilton. Jim, the teacher, shrugged his shoulders in disappointment.

"Another Sunday morning down the tubes," he complained. "Four of us meeting out of a potential of hundreds."

"What's wrong with this class?" Sandy asked. "Why don't people come and get involved?"

There was a moment of silence as the four thought about this question.

"Listen," Jim said finally. "I've got an idea!"

"Shoot!" Paul encouraged him. "We're willing to help in any way we can."

Jim got up and walked over to the chalkboard on the wall. "First of all, we have no objectives in this class. What I mean is, what are we doing here? What is this Sunday School class trying to accomplish? Let's make a list on the board. Paul, what exactly do you think an adult Sunday School is all about? Vicki and Sandy, what do you think? Let's be clear about what we're trying to do before we try to do it!"

"As far as I'm concerned," Paul spoke up, "our Sunday School class is a waste of time to me if it doesn't contribute to my growth as a believer in Jesus Christ." Jim, Sandy and Vicki nodded in agreement. "The overall goal for our class must be Christian maturity."

"I think you're right," Sandy said, "but isn't the goal of Christian maturity a little broad? Can't we be more specific in our thinking?"

Basically, the adult division of Sunday School has four main objectives it is trying to accomplish. These are:
1. To reach prospective class members.
2. To produce an atmosphere of warmth and acceptance.
3. To provide sound biblical instruction.
4. To promote daily application of biblical material.

Each objective, of course, is partially determined by the other three. You cannot have sound biblical instruction unless you have class members to instruct. And you cannot reach prospective members unless the atmosphere within your class makes them want to become active participants. Each objective, then, partially depends on the others for fulfillment.

"We're on the right track!" Jim exclaimed. "Now let's find out a little more about each of these objectives."

TO REACH PROSPECTIVE CLASS MEMBERS

It may seem elementary to say that one must have pupils in order to have a school, but many churches have no planned program for reaching and for recruiting prospective class members at all! They seem to assume that it is the teacher's responsibility to attract new members, while some teachers obviously operate upon the assumption that the pupils in his class will bring their friends and acquaintances. And others take it for granted that the real key to Sunday School growth lies with the pastor. So we all tend to look at one another, pass the buck and stagnate.

"That's one of the real problems with this class," Paul lamented. "I admit that I haven't invited anyone to Sunday School in a long time. But I guess the problem is that I don't know how to do it. I always get tongue-tied when I try to invite someone to church or Sunday School."

"My problem is different," said Sandy. "I just don't know where to meet people who would be good prospects for this class."

"I guess I'm just lazy," Vicki admitted. "I know plenty of

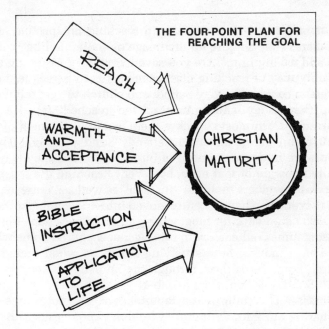

THE FOUR-POINT PLAN FOR REACHING THE GOAL

REACH

WARMTH AND ACCEPTANCE

BIBLE INSTRUCTION

APPLICATION TO LIFE

CHRISTIAN MATURITY

people who should be in this class, but I just don't take the time or energy to go and invite them."

Jim made a list on the chalkboard that read like this:

Problems in Reaching New Class Members:

1. Inability to witness on a one-to-one basis.

2. Lack of confrontation with people who would be potential members.

3. Lack of discipline in spending time inviting people to Sunday School.

"There are ways to reach prospective class members," Jim offered. "Success in a Sunday School doesn't happen by accident. Let's think about some of these ways to reach people."

Prospective class members are reached basically in one of two ways: by an individual or by the class as a whole. Many people feel panicky, like Paul Hamilton, when someone starts talking about individual responsibility in reaching prospective class members. They conjure up the image of "buttonholing" someone and asking him, "Are you saved, brother?" assuming that the only way of reaching class members is to persuade unbelievers to come to Sunday School and church to "get religion."

But the Sunday School must reach the "reached" as well as the "unreached." In most churches there is a large segment of the adult membership that never attends Sunday School. These people are in desperate need of Sunday School. (They may be totally unaware of that need, however.) Reaching the prospective class members includes "inreach" as well as "outreach."

Believers who have recently moved into a new neighborhood are also candidates for membership in Sunday School. People are sometimes rather slow in finding a new church home when they have moved; how satisfying it can be when their new church home finds them through the ministry of a concerned adult Sunday School class member!

This is not to minimize the importance of personal evangelism or sharing our faith with those who don't know Jesus Christ as Lord and Saviour. But it should be remembered that believers and church members who don't attend Sunday School are to be considered prospective class members too.

"Let's make a list of the possibilities," Jim encouraged. He wrote the following on the board:

The "Reached" We Need to Reach:

1. Church members who do not attend Sunday School on a regular basis.

2. Believers in the neighborhood who do not attend a church regularly.

3. New neighbors in the community who are believers.

Reaching the "Unreached"

Another way to reach prospective class members is for individuals to share their faith with unbelievers, lead them to a saving knowledge of the Lord Jesus Christ, and bring them to Sunday

School and church as a natural follow-up. These new babes in Christ will need the spiritual nurture provided by our Sunday School classes and the fellowship with other believers.

The fact that personal evangelism is a frightening experience for some Christians may indicate that our churches have not been equipping us for performing this ministry of "...the word of reconciliation." Often people are too uncomfortable with the other members of their class to share these difficulties and fears of witnessing and living a Christian life; there is a fear of appearing "unspiritual" in the eyes of our fellow class members.

But the fact remains that personal evangelism is a vital means of reaching prospective class members, and our Sunday School classes should be equipping members to do this very thing!

Reaching Through Visitation

"Well, we've decided we need to reach the 'reached' and the 'unreached,' " Jim said. "But our class has no organized method to do so."

"Visitation!" one of the young women remarked. "Let's talk about a visitation program!"

An effective visitation program is vital to the Sunday School. Several class members or one or two couples can help reach prospective class members by taking one or two evenings in the week to seek out and fellowship with these people. When the joy, warmth and compassion of Christ are expressed in initial encounters with prospective class members, they will be highly motivated to accept the invitation to attend a Sunday School class and church. The prospects will be much more inclined to attend because they won't feel like total strangers the first time they come; there will be several familiar faces among the new group of people.

Visitation after the first-time guests attend the Sunday School is helpful also. It insures a second return and shows the guests that they are sincerely wanted. Too often a class's visitation program melts after the first encounter, leaving the prospective members up in the air. Follow-through on visitation is just as important as the initial visit.

"Okay," Jim said, "we've got a good start. I'm going to write on the board all the things we can do to reach prospective class members."

Reaching Prospective Class Members:

1. Contact people in the church who do not attend a Sunday School class.

2. Contact new residents in the community who may not know of your particular church.

3. Contact believers in the community who do not have a church home as yet.

4. Set up a regular, systematic visitation program.

5. Encourage and teach individual witnessing to bring others to Christ—and then to church and Sunday School.

"Objective Number One," Jim stated, "has been agreed upon. We need to be reaching prospective class members. Now for Objective Number Two: What do we do to make sure that these new members continue to come to our Sunday School class?"

"Good question!" Paul agreed. "We've had so many people come to class one time and then disappear off the face of the earth. What are we doing wrong?"

"Maybe it has something to do with the atmosphere in the class," Sandy ventured. "Maybe we ought to make them feel more comfortable than we do."

"I agree," Jim said. "And I think that should be the second objective for our Sunday School."

TO PRODUCE AN ATMOSPHERE
OF WARMTH AND ACCEPTANCE

Each individual has basic personal needs which can be met by other human beings. It has been observed that three of these needs are: (1) the need for attention, (2) the need for acceptance, and (3) the need for affirmation.

Recognizing Modern Isolation

A great deal in contemporary society prevents the satisfaction of these needs. Computer-age technology tends to obscure one's individual identity behind a pattern of numbers on an IBM card. Approximately 27 percent of the population of the U.S. moves its residence every year, leaving friends and associates behind again and again. Sociologists state that this mobility results in people being set adrift on a sea of anonymity. Loneliness and a feeling of isolation have become characteristics of modern existence, and people don't like it.

Loving Away Isolation

The Lord Jesus told His disciples that love is the sure sign of discipleship (see John 13:35). And the love of which He was speaking is "a love springing from a sense of the preciousness of the object loved."[1] Loving people means paying attention to them, not being indifferent toward them. Loving people means accepting them in spite of their problems and personality quirks. Loving people means affirming them, encouraging them where they are rather than rejecting them for their imperfections. The people in the church of Jesus Christ should do much to meet in a Christian manner the basic needs of the individuals in their fellowship.

"This raises some interesting questions," Jim remarked. "Let's write them down."

1. Are we producing an atmosphere of warmth and acceptance?

2. How do people feel as they enter our Sunday School classroom?

3. Do they feel a part of the group?

4. Do they feel welcome?

5. Do they receive positive attention from the group?

6. Do they leave with a feeling of personal worth and a sense that they have been recognized and appreciated as individuals?

7. Or do they feel like intruders or outsiders?

8. Are they confronted with open "fellowship groups" or impenetrable "spiritual cliques"?

There should be an understanding among the class members that any visitors will be warmly accepted by all. The conditions which produce the needed atmosphere of warmth and acceptance can be planned and arranged for. They usually do not happen by accident. Prayerful consideration should be given as to what can be done to give each individual a sense of being precious in both the sight of God and other class members.

"Wow!" exclaimed Sandy. "Now there's an objective we really need to be working toward!"

"Right," answered Jim. "It seems to me that if our Sunday School can meet these two objectives, it will be on its way to being the tool of God that He wants it to be."

"But let's not stop here," Paul urged. "There are several other objectives we need to be concerned with."

TO PROVIDE SOUND BIBLICAL INSTRUCTION

"Well, this objective mainly concerns me," Jim decided. "I'm the teacher. And I guess I've got a lot to learn about how God can use me in that role. But you know something? I'm more excited about teaching my class now than I have been in a long time."

"Okay, let's go on, then," Vicki said. "We've decided that Sunday School needs to reach prospective class members and make them feel accepted. But how does the Sunday School teach them the truths of the Bible?"

Depending upon the Holy Spirit

It is the teacher's job to bring forth the particular Bible truths that a class is studying on any given Sunday. But it must be remembered that it is the Holy Spirit who makes that truth real in a class member's life. Once the teacher recognizes this fact, he will be freed from the pressure of having to "pound the truth" into his pupils' heads. He will learn to rely, through prayer and preparation, upon the power and thoroughness of the Holy Spirit.

As the teacher opens himself to the Spirit's teaching ability, he will discover previously unknown powers and talents. He will see results in the lives of his pupils that will assure him of God's presence in the classroom.

The Holy Spirit, then, teaches both the teacher and the students. Only He can provide the sound biblical instruction that is necessary in Sunday School.

Minimizing Lecture Method

It needs to be recognized that sound biblical instruction means more than a mini-preaching service. The old teaching adage of "you sit still while I instill" doesn't work when it comes to providing the best conditions for adult learning.

The teacher who lectures to his class for the entire session runs the risk of losing his students' attention. Adults need to be challenged and confronted in the classroom into thinking through problems and offering solutions to them.

The exclusive use of the lecture method of teaching prevents a difference of opinion and viewpoint. Although someone in the class may have a valid interpretation or opinion, it is often left unsaid because there just isn't enough time to fit it in before, during or after the teacher's lecture.

Finally, recollection of material given during a lecture period is much lower than it is with group participation. Statistics show that retention is significantly related to the amount of discussion and involvement the pupil has in the lesson.

Sound biblical instruction, then, is best achieved when the teacher seeks to actively involve his class members in the learning process.

Relying upon Group Participation

Since the Holy Spirit indwells each Christian in a Sunday School class, the class member is capable of making as valid a contribution to the learning experience as the teacher is. It is necessary to make room in the classroom procedure for meaningful learning experiences such as discussion, buzz groups, circle response, neighbor-nudging and other forms of personal interaction among the various class members. Subsequent chapters in this book offer in-depth information regarding effective adult teaching/learning methods.

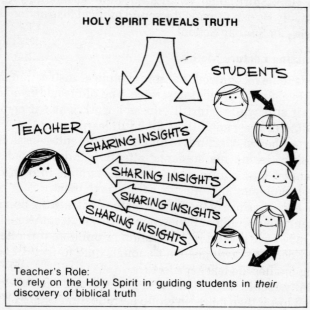

HOLY SPIRIT REVEALS TRUTH

STUDENTS

TEACHER

SHARING INSIGHTS

SHARING INSIGHTS

SHARING INSIGHTS

SHARING INSIGHTS

Teacher's Role:
to rely on the Holy Spirit in guiding students in *their* discovery of biblical truth

Jim was amazed. "This sheds a whole new light on teaching. I always thought a good teacher prepared a lesson during the week and then told it to the class on Sunday morning. I guess I never realized how much better it would be if everyone participated."

"And maybe that's why I feel like I don't really know what some of the other class members think," offered Sandy. "They never really do any of the talking."

"But there's one more objective," Paul stated. "I always forget the lesson when I walk out of Sunday School. Shouldn't we be applying the lessons in our day-to-day lives?"

"I think you're right, Paul," Jim agreed. "Let's make that our final objective for adult Sunday School."

TO PROMOTE DAILY APPLICATION OF BIBLICAL MATERIAL

What happens after the dismissal bell rings on Sunday morning? Sunday School is officially over and too often that ends it all. Class members venture forth from their classrooms with nothing but a nice warm feeling which they hope will sustain them until next week—same time, same station. Should Sunday School affect the lives of people through the week? Or does God intend the precious truth of His Word to remain locked up within the hearts and minds of His people?

Encouraging Faith to Work

The answer to this, of course, is that Monday through Saturday should be affected by what has taken place on Sunday morning.

But many times people have stumbled into the pitfall of which James warns them. It is deceptive to think that what takes place in the classroom is all that really matters. James exhorts Christians to be "doers of the word and not hearers only." Spiritual maturity and the love of Christ need to be expressed in concrete ways. James says that faith must be expressed in good works. "Even so faith, if it hath not works, is dead, being alone," and "...faith without works is dead."

Each individual class member must be able to actively express his faith in the Lord Jesus Christ. Personal evangelism, visiting the sick and bereaved, assisting the elderly and other service projects should be the natural outgrowth of and response to the sound biblical instruction in our classes. The Sunday School must provide the framework in which the truth of God's Word can be concretely expressed.

Encouraging Faith to Grow

The outcome of promoting application of God's Word in class members' individual lives is that faith is increased. And as faith in Jesus Christ is increased, more and more people will be brought into God's kingdom by the witness of Sunday School adult members. As faith grows, the atmosphere of warmth and acceptance will become a natural part of Sunday School classroom environments. The circle of Sunday School objectives will be complete. Those who are brought to class as prospects will have the opportunity to become total disciples of Jesus Christ. They will have an opportunity to love and care for others and to melt the feelings of isolation which are so prevalent. But these opportunities will come only when biblical instruction is sound and made applicable to the pupils' daily lives.

READY...SET...GO!

"Well, that does it!" Jim exclaimed. "Those are the four objectives of the adult Sunday School."

"Those are four specific aims which will definitely result in Christian growth—our overall objective," Sandy added. "It's exciting to know where we're going."

"And why," Vicki said.

"We're on the right track," Jim cautioned, "but we're not through by any means. We still have a lot to learn about adult Sunday School."

"Say, I have an idea!" Vicki said. "Why don't you and Sandy come over Tuesday night and we'll tackle the next step in organizing this class."

It was unanimous. The Taylors and Hamiltons finalized the time of the Tuesday night meeting, closed their Sunday School class with prayer, asking God to guide them in their upcoming meeting, and proceeded on to the worship service.

They had discovered that when a Sunday School knows

where it is going, it is much easier to get there! And they were on their way!

SOME QUESTIONS TO CONSIDER

1. List a few specific reasons for having an adult Sunday School.

2. How is your class presently involved in reaching new members? How could you improve your "outreach" and "in-reach" ministries?

3. Does your class presently provide a warm and accepting atmosphere? If so, how is it accomplished? If not, list three ways you could improve.

4. What ways do you employ to encourage your class members to apply the Sunday School lesson to their weekday lives?

FOOTNOTE

1. Kenneth S. Wuest, *Golden Nuggets from the Greek New Testament* (Grand Rapids: Wm. B. Eerdmans Publishing Company, 1940), p. 63.

How to Recognize an Adult

What is an adult? How would you describe adulthood? Is adulthood indicated by the development of sexual maturity? Does a person become an adult when he reaches a certain age? Some educators and psychologists place adulthood at 21, others at 24 and some at 18.

No one criterion is sufficient to define adulthood. Paul Maves suggests that a person is an adult when he can answer a majority of these questions with a yes:

Has he reached his legal age?

Has he finished his schooling?

Does he live away from the parental home?

Is he self-supporting financially?

Does he make his own decisions?

Is he married?

Does he carry adult responsibilities?

Does he look upon himself as an adult, is he accepted as one by other adults, and does he seek the company of other adults?[1]

These questions seem to indicate that adulthood is not defined by any single characteristic or a number of characteristics considered in isolation. Adulthood is a grouping of characteristics. A person is an adult when he becomes personally accountable for himself and accepts adult responsibilities.

Age is one ingredient of adulthood. It usually indicates some level of education achieved and a possible range of experience. Age is definitely related to a person's role and function in his community. The ability to obtain a marriage license without parental approval, eligibility for voting and other functions clearly indicate the relationship between age and adulthood.

Maturity is another word associated with adulthood. But maturity is progressive and varies within different individuals. Reuel Howe has characterized the mature person as "one who is able to meet his own inner impulses as well as more obvious attacks from without. This person is able to maintain a proper balance between work and play. Being mature involves being able to accept one's own and the opposite sex. It is also being able to establish a relationship that is mutually fulfilling to both. The mature person is one who is able to express his love for others while at the same time becoming less dependent upon being loved himself."[2]

Douglas Heath suggests that a mature person is one who has a level of stability within his life. He is able to resist and recover from disorganizing experiences and situations and maintain a sense of his own identity. He can cope with new experiences and information without being unduly threatened. He is able to integrate the new into his own life. He faces the social world realistically and, because he recognizes his own biases, attempts to avoid judging everything in terms of his own needs. The mature person maintains a level of flexibility and is able to explore a variety of possible solutions and their consequences. He is also somewhat autonomous.[3]

For the Christian, maturity also includes the individual's relation to God and Jesus Christ. This is not just something that is tacked onto life. It is not an optional extra which some people choose. It is more like the sugar which disappears in a cup of coffee but which sweetens all of it. Paul says, "We should no longer be babes...but, lovingly attached to truth, we should grow up in every way toward Him who is the Head—Christ"

(Eph. 4:14,15, *MLB*). "I once more suffer birthpains until Christ is formed within you" (Gal. 4:19, *MLB*).

In this sense the genuine adult Sunday School teacher must be an evangelist at heart. He knows that unless Christ is "all and in all" life at best is barren and bitter. And he will look for opportunities in every teaching situation to point his pupils to the Lamb of God that takes away the sin of the world (see John 1:29).

Occupation is another important factor in the definition of adulthood. Society generally expects that adults engage in some type of gainful employment—teacher, plumber, housewife, salesman or some other occupation. Because an adult spends so much of his time working, his occupation can become a central factor in his life. It can affect what he does and thinks and what others think and feel about him. Part of an adult's identity is tied to his occupation.

An adult's *interests* and *attitudes* are expected to be stable because of the breadth of his experience. His interests center primarily around his occupation, family, political party, church and community organizations. An adult realizes that many changes need to be made in society, but those changes will not come about instantly. His beliefs and attitudes tend to be more conservative than those of youth and may become more stable or dogmatic as he gets older.

An adult's *social role* is another important part of adulthood. Society expects an adult to do and accomplish certain things. He is expected to be responsible for his own family and to serve his community in some way. He is expected to assume roles involving both responsibility and accountability.

Adulthood is the widest age range of any of the defined periods of life. Once a person becomes an adult, he remains in that classification until death. But adulthood is not static. Changes take place and certain characteristics emerge at different periods during this phase of life. Because of these changes, adulthood is usually divided into three periods: young adulthood, middle adulthood and older adulthood.

YOUNG ADULTS ARE DIFFERENT

Who are today's young adults? Young adulthood actually includes several groups—collegians, newly married couples and adults in their early 30s. And each of these groups has different interests and needs. For the purpose of this book, the age range for young adulthood is approximately 18 (or high school graduate) to 35. Let's look at some of the responsibilities facing the young adults to whom you minister.

The College Age Young Adult (18-23)

College age young people are young adults. Their adult responsibilities are broadening rapidly, such as being able to vote when they turn 18. Most churches, however, continue to think of collegians as older youth and include them in their youth activities. Some collegians are closer in maturity to high school students than to adulthood, yet many have assumed the status of adult.

In discussing the college age young adult, we must differentiate between the person who attends college and the person who works at a job. The college age person who is working at the age of 18 may be more mature than the 20-year-old who has not worked but has attended college for two years. The working young adult and the student live in two different worlds. They associate with different types of people each day. Many of their interests are different. One is work-oriented, the other is study-oriented. The working young adult works in a structured setting where he must answer to those above him. The student is more or less on his own and responsible for his own use of time.

In spite of these differences, young adults—whether working or attending school—do have some purposes and goals in common. Freedman and Sanford have suggested four characteristics that apply to all young adults.

First, college age young adults are usually seeking to stabilize their sex identity, to learn sex roles and to achieve psychological intimacy. Sex for the collegian is "here and now." Many feel that love and sex are for the present without the need for lasting commitments. Even trial marriages are a thing of the past because living together is no longer viewed as preparation for marriage.

Second, college age young adults experience a definite increase in "rebellious independence."

Third, they are moving from an authoritarian way of life to a more relative outlook on life.

Fourth, they tend to become more expressive in their human relationships (especially in the area of sex, as already mentioned) and are more open to excitement and newness.[4]

The Young Adult (24-35)

For the most part young adults are urban and mobile. They are very independent and are searching for something new. They don't always know what they are searching for, but they want life to be different and better than what they have seen in the previous generation. They react against the impersonalism of being lost in the crowd, yet they are still a part of this life-style.

The values of the past generation are not binding upon young adults. They hesitate to take what they are told at face value, especially if it comes from institutions and those who represent their "growing up" world. In a sense they are attempting to carve out their own world with its own customs, values and beliefs, yet still retain some remnant of the past world. They make demands and expect results. Most young adults, however, are willing to work to bring changes in the present system.

Young adults experience a new freedom. Former rules, "what will others think?" and "thou shalt nots," are meaningless as tools of enforced conformity and manipulation. They will do as they please, how they please and stand up to the voice of authority with shouts of "why?" "no" and "there is a better way than what you are offering."

Questions that have been asked through the centuries are still being asked by young adults today. Who am I? Where am I going? How can I get the most out of life? How do I break away from this conformity and rat race? Dr. Clifford Anderson has suggested that young adults can be classified by three words: liberated, skeptical and searching.[5]

Responsibilities of Young Adulthood

Selecting a Mate ■ Selecting a mate is one of the most important and long-reaching decisions a person will ever make in his lifetime. The person selected as a mate must be more than just a physical or sexual partner. This means that time and careful consideration are important ingredients in making this choice. The Christian's philosophy is going to be at odds with that of society, because marriage for him involves whether or not the choice is God's choice and the marriage relationship is to be a permanent one.

Many young adults marry during the unstable years of later youth or very early adulthood. Some purposely postpone marriage until they reach their 30s. Others marry while they are continuing their education which means both partners will probably have to work and adjustments will have to be made in terms of finances, time and postponement of a family.

Those who do not marry make that decision for a variety of reasons. Finances, not finding just "the right one," not wanting to assume the responsibilities of family life, change in sexual attitudes and morals are a few of the reasons.

Learning to Live with a Marriage Partner ■ "Marriage," says Dr. Robert Shaper, "is a total commitment of a total person for total life."[6] It is shocking to see the lack of preparation for this "total commitment." A person spends close to 20 years in preparation for his vocation which in most cases will last for as long as the person is alive or employable. A marriage which should last equally as long is entered into with a minimum or even no preparation—and people are surprised when marriages fail! Marriage is the process of learning to live together and it is a continuous process.

Before the ceremony a young adult should seriously analyze his motivation for getting married. Why marriage? Why this person? What do I expect to get and give to the marriage relationship? Many have not asked this question nor have their churches assisted them in this regard.

It is imperative that the church's ministry to young adults include adequate (even mandatory) premarital counseling. Sunday School classes for young married couples dealing specifically with the marriage relationship should also be a vital part of the church's ministry. A church that does not give thorough, honest and relevant assistance on the five major marital problems—communication, sex, finances, in-laws and spiritual/religious problems—fails in its ministry. Other problems such as child raising, social life, work roles and the scriptural pattern for Christian marriage are also important topics, which should be covered in a pre-marital and marital teaching/counseling ministry.

Starting a Family ■ Celebration, happiness, joy, excitement, interruption of routine, abrupt changes, adjustments—these words describe something of what occurs at the start of family life. Many parents eagerly anticipate the arrival of their new member and make preparations together. Others are overcome with fear, dread or resentment. For many the start of a family was carefully planned. But for others the arrival of a child was not expected and perhaps not even wanted. Wise counsel by the church's pastor and family physician during premarital counseling will assist in the fulfillment of this task. Preparation for child raising and care should begin well before the child arrives. A realistic knowledge of what starting a family involves will help the couple make the necessary adjustments.

How well do your young adult programs help class members through this phase of their lives? Do you provide adequate counseling, teaching, library resources and people willing to help when the need arises?

Rearing Children ■ Once a baby is born he is totally dependent upon his parents. The type of family life he will have depends upon the parents' background and their sharing of roles and work in the home. A child will have many needs and make many demands upon the parents who may or may not be capable of responding in a positive manner.

Who is responsible for rearing these children? The mother or the father? Is it reasonable to expect both of them to be equally involved? Adherence to the teaching of the Scriptures will lead to a positive fulfillment of this important function of young adulthood.

Managing a Home ■ Young adults, at an increasingly early age, begin to establish their own households. This is true for the single as well as the married.

Managing a home involves selecting a place to live, whether to rent or buy, furniture, utilities, cleaning, buying food, paying bills, entertaining in the home, etc. The division of labor and cooperative effort should be clearly defined and agreed upon by both partners.

The adult's financial status will affect the type of home he chooses and where the home will be located. Couples who feel they must immediately buy the best and most modern appliances and gadgets on credit will face difficulties and pressures that can disrupt their entire marriage. The credit plan of managing a home appears easy, but long-range planning and learning to wait is safer.

Occupational Involvement ■ Working 40 years in one occupation may sound like a fulfilled life but if the person has hated his work all that time his life may have been empty. It is estimated that a large segment of the working population is unhappy in its present occupations.

With unstable economic conditions and inflation continually increasing, families try to earn more money forcing many women into the labor force of the nation. If a position is offered that will bring extra income, many adults do not hesitate to leave a job and even to move to a different area of the country to accept the new position. For the young couple with no children it is easy to move about. Because of this you may find a significant turnover in the membership of your class.

Many men and women who have trained for a specific profession or position are disappointed upon completion of their training. They may not be satisfied with that type of employment or find the labor market overstocked.

The young adult's vocation may assume out-of-proportion importance as he strives for financial security, status or personal satisfaction. This in turn will affect his involvement and faithfulness to a local church. The church, for many young married couples, is last on their list of priorities because they are caught up in planning and building for themselves. The church will have to go out to them and not wait for them to come to the church. Individual class members are the dynamic force to reach their own peers.

Adequate fulfillment of this responsibility is necessary for one's own self-image and has a bearing on the fulfillment of other responsibilities. Vocational fulfillment is tied to seeking God's will and plan for the individual life. The Christian young adult will have many questions which the church can help to answer and explore.

Finding a Social Group ■ The young adult in school has many social opportunities. But for the single adult who is employed, social involvement may be limited to those at work. The increase of computer dating services and single apartment dwellings, which are cities in themselves reserved for singles, reflect this drive and desire for social contact. Churches which provide a varied and interesting program can minister to many young adults who might otherwise have no desire to become involved with the church.

The married couple may find themselves cut off from former friends who are single or married and busy with their own lives. The arrival of children, living in a new or limited environment, or limited finances may curtail social contacts which are very necessary for the young adult's total development. Young married adult and single adult classes which provide for the social as well as the educational and spiritual needs can produce an abundance of young adult leadership.

MIDDLE-AGED ADULTS NEED UNDERSTANDING

Middle-aged or middle adulthood refers to the period between young adulthood and old age. Although it is difficult to set precise chronological limits, middle age is generally thought of as extending from age 35 to 60 or 65.

Responsibilities of Middle-aged Adults

Civic and Social Responsibility ■ Middle-aged adults bring stability to the area of civic and social life. During early adulthood participation and membership in community, church and business groups tend to be low, but they reach their peak in middle age. Many middle adults have a greater appreciation for their social relationships and more freedom to devote to these activities.

There appear to be several reasons for this increase in social and civic life. Both men and women are more established in their vocations and there are fewer family members to look after as the children grow up and leave home. Increased leisure time, the need for a definite purpose in life and the need to feel creative and useful also contribute to increased involvement in community life. The middle-age adult brings to these activities his years of experience in making decisions and a wide range of life experiences. His status in the community lends a stabilizing force to civic and social organizations. In this way the committed Christian can be an influence for Christ in these activities.

Establishing and Maintaining Economic Stability ▪ This task has many sides. Many adults reach the peak of their earning power during middle age which places some of them in positions of prominence and continual advancement. But at the same time financial demands are increasing and often overwhelming—purchase and upkeep of a home, retirement funds, college education for the children and money for emergencies. If the adult has reached the peak of his earning power with little chance for advancement in sight and the cost of living continues to increase, frustration and discouragement may build. Boredom and dissatisfaction may lead him to search for a new position. This brings a new set of problems because the employment market is unstable. Changing technology and types of jobs may necessitate months and years of retraining.

Some men take on extra jobs hoping to make ends meet. In other families the mother enters or rejoins the working world. If this development task is not reached with some degree of accomplishment it may interfere with the enrichment of other areas of life. On the other hand, success and devotion to a job that brings great satisfaction may also take a man away from his family, church and community responsibilities.

This is the age of accountability. "An adult of middle age comes to realize that his life values have been valid, or he realizes that they are invalid and that to hold on to them would be fruitless. Either he has achieved most of his material or vocational goals, or he will not reach them. His job will become more secure because of his skill and experience, or more insecure as his skill becomes obsolete and work is more difficult to find and to hold....Educational goals are either completed or they will not be attained. If a middle adult faces unfulfilled goals with little hope of accomplishing them, he must either seek new goals and interests that can be achieved, or remain frustrated and defeated."[7]

Especially in the Christian life, many adults find themselves in the doldrums. They lack joy. They are powerless. They have stopped witnessing. Millions of empty seats in our churches belong to "used-to-go Christians." The seats should never have become empty. Prevention is easier than surgery. But, in every community, apathy and indifference have already infected adults. Here, the orders of the day are: (1) make your adult department what it should be; (2) pray and work for revived, activated class members; (3) start a thorough, widespread and continuing evangelistic program—outreach, ingathering, rehabilitation, more outreach!

Guiding Teenagers to Adulthood ■ During middle age adults usually have children that are in their teens or close to adulthood, or they do not have children. It is an adjustment period for the children as they reach into teens or adulthood and for the parents. It is a time of emerging independence on the part of the children versus continued domination or a grudging relinquishment of the relationship by the parents. It is a difficult task but a rewarding one for parents who succeed in making their own adjustment as well as helping their teenagers adjust.

Many more persons are converted as young people than as adults. Do your adults pray, as families and as a Sunday School class, for the salvation of their sons and daughters? How can Christian parents help to bring about their conversion? Many, by their silence or their blundering, contribute to the lostness of the upcoming generation. And many are looking for a church that offers assistance to homes in which the generation gap is widening.

Leisure Time Activities ■ Many middle-aged adults have an increasing amount of leisure time, thanks to increasing affluence and the shortened work week. How this time is used varies depending upon past activities and possibilities for the future. Many adults cling to old interests in place of seeking new ones. If older interests lack the former satisfaction, the adult selects one which gives him the greatest pleasure. Less strenuous hobbies and activities come to the forefront now. Their interests narrow and shift from large group activities to the small group of close friends. Quieter activities such as hobbies, collecting things, dinner parties, study groups, adult education classes, travel and leisurely outings take precedence. Adults in the church will either find satisfaction there in terms of their interests, hobbies or service, or will seek their recreation and learning activities elsewhere. Can you list six activities or programs that your church offers that meet the needs of your adults' leisure time? Have you asked them what they would like your church or class to provide? In what way would they be willing to help?

Husband-Wife Relationships ▪ Middle age has been labeled "the dangerous age." When the children leave home, the house seems empty and the couple must learn to adjust to one another in a new way. Often the companionship of one's mate seems insufficient. The waning physical drive carries with it serious psychological effects. Often the man has an urge to have a fling or prove his manliness. The flirtations of adolescence may begin to appear once again. A high rate of divorce is found among adults in their 40s and 50s.

Other couples, however, experience a deepening of their relationships because of the opportunity to devote more time to one another. They learn to depend more upon each other and help each other adjust to the changes that occur during this period. This developmental task requires considerable work and flexibility, but the rewards are great.

Accepting and Adjusting to Physical Changes ▪ Perhaps the greatest amount of concern over middle age revolves around changes in the biological or physical realm. These changes become more and more apparent with age and there is no escaping or reversing them. Middle adults usually have less energy and strength and their sexual powers begin to diminish. The tendency to gain weight, to lose hair and watch it slowly become gray, is inevitable. Skin texture changes, bringing a coarser appearance and wrinkles.

During the menopause, which occurs in the 40s or early 50s, the woman loses her reproductive function. The time of life during which the reproductive capacity terminates has been called the "climacteric" which means "peak" or "climax." The changes that take place during the climacteric can cause difficulties in relationships, adjustments and psychological equilibrium.

Circulatory difficulties occur and the glands gradually become sluggish. Hypertension and heart complications are common, as well as digestive and elimination problems. The physical senses begin to decline in the latter part of middle age. Partial hearing loss and impaired vision are common. The senses of touch and taste are not as keen as earlier. Illnesses and disease are more in evidence. A person's mental processes may slow down, but the older belief of severe mental decline is a myth. It may take longer for an adult to learn, but his capacity for learning and thinking remains. The physical changes taking place can greatly affect the adult's attitudes and emotions. It is easy for him to slide into a process of psychological deterioration. Depression, insecurity and self-depreciation are frequent.

A person's preparation for this state of life has a great effect upon how he reacts to middle adulthood. A maturing faith that is continually growing and deepening will provide the necessary stability for meeting changes. In order to adjust to the physical or psychological changes, he needs to maintain the ability to be flexible and to anticipate change and growth. Wide self-involvement instead of retreating is an important key. Fulfilling the needs of others brings greater adjustment. The ability to accept, adjust and look forward to any change, whether physical, mental or environmental must begin in early adulthood and continue if middle age is to be meaningful.

Adjusting to One's Own Parents ■ Often the responsibility for one's parents must be assumed during this time of life. Some adults take their aging parents into their own home to live with them, others support their parents in a rest home or help them maintain their own residence nearby. There are two directions in which these relationships can move. For some adults, tremendous problems are created when the two families live under one roof. Others are able to make the necessary adjustments. A good adjustment, however, depends largely on the kind of parent-child relationship that was established many years before.

This is middle age, a time of change and challenge. As one writer says, "Thus, middle age should properly be regarded as a time of accomplishment and rewards, of early ambitions fulfilled, of involvement with a world for which we have, in our turn, become responsible. In short, these have to be the prime years of our lives."[8] The church can play a vital role in helping adults find meaning for the middle years.

WORKING WITH OLDER ADULTS

Old age is enjoyed by millions today. By 1985 it is expected that the United States will have an over '65' population of 25 million! Longer life expectancy has been a major goal for centuries. Today we have it—a condition now taken for granted and at times even considered a social problem. In a youth-oriented society the older adult sometimes feels like excess baggage. Society has a tendency to look upon older adults in terms of what they have been and what they have *accomplished* instead of what they are and *can* do!

How can old age be defined? Perhaps "older adulthood" is a more realistic term, for many older adults are still capable of functioning, contributing to and receiving from life. Older adulthood begins at about 60 or the time of retirement. Not all in this age group seek retirement, however. Many continue to work as they have in earlier years or work on their own.

Many individual differences exist within this age group as

with the other age groups. Barron in *The Aging American* has described old age as follows:

1. There is an "early-late maturity" between 65 and 70 years of age, where there is generally a little psychological fatigue, a marked alteration in skin dryness, no marked deterioration physiologically, no withdrawal from the community, and no marked habit alterations of differences in needs.

2. There is a "middle-late maturity" between 70 and 75 years of age, when generally there is a marked slump in energy, recovery rate, reaction time, social participation, participation in the labor force, flexibility, freedom from chronic ailments, and an increase in fatigue and mental disorders.

3. There is a "late-late maturity" from 75 years of age and up. During this time there generally is a uniform picture of little energy, fatigue, a high incidence of ailments likely to be terminal, deeply lined skin, a general withdrawal from community life and little zest.[9]

Adjustments for Older Adults

There are several adjustments older adults must make. An understanding of these adjustments will help you minister to older adults more effectively.

Physical Adjustments ▪ One of the easily recognized characteristics of older adulthood is physical decline. Older adults are usually susceptible to cancer, diseases of the heart, arthritic and rheumatic ailments, diseases of the brain and nervous system. Physical changes and problems affect vision, hearing, balance, teeth, skeleton, muscles, the digestive system, circulatory system, nervous system, weight loss or gain, hair loss and color, skin, sexual desire, hygiene problems and other degenerative process of the body. One writer has suggested that "one does not die of old age, but of disease."[10]

Some people paint a dismal picture of old age indicating that 80 percent of adults over 65 living at home have one or more chronic health problems. The American National Red Cross, however, has suggested that "many old people are affected very little by the chronic illnesses that are associated with aging. Most individuals proceed confidently into old age, maintaining their health, alertness and interests to life's end."

Economic Adjustment and Retirement ■ A person's work and profession in life is very important to him. He directs much of his energy and creativity toward his work. His closest friends and his status in the community are often tied solely to his work.

Retirement changes that picture. The switch from work to nonwork may leave an overwhelming vacuum in the person's life unless he has carefully prepared for the change. "When one no longer has a steady job, he tends to feel that he is no longer contributing to society, that he has lost his sense of worth, that he is 'just retired'... and that he is caught in a retirement trap and unable to cope with leisure because all he knows by experience and mental orientation is how to work." Self-esteem can suffer greatly during this adjustment.[11]

One of the major adjustments in retirement is the amount of income available to the older adult. Those who have planned and prepared, have adequate retirement programs or wealthy children to support them, have little need to worry. The unfortunate part of a retirement income is that it usually remains stable while the cost of living continues to climb. Many do not receive an adequate stipend and thus become so limited and boxed in that there is really little hope of improving their living standards.

Again it must be emphasized that attitude toward aging and retirement, in addition to advance preparation, forms the basis for adjustment and fulfillment of the remaining years. For many these are enjoyable and happy years because they continue to reach out to others and to society. An extensive church program including a Sunday School class may bring these adults to center their lives around the church.

Adjusting to Loss of Loved Ones ▪ Death is a separating force. Many couples anticipate spending their retirement years together. Then suddenly one is no longer there. Women experience this much more than men for there are approximately twice as many widows as widowers. Most of these widows remain single.

When death occurs decisions must be made. "Shall I continue to live alone? Where shall I move? What about living with the children? What about a retirement home? What can my church offer me now? I've never handled money before and I don't know what to do. How can I learn how to cook at this age?"

After the death of one's mate loneliness sets in. There are fewer friends at this age and perhaps fewer social functions. And now the death of the spouse! The remaining mate feels terribly alone. But loneliness is just one of the emotional aspects of aging. M. Gitelson has suggested six different patterns of emotional adjustment in old age.

1. A decreased memory for recent events—turning away from the painfulness of the present.

2. A sharpness of memory for the past.

3. A more self-assertive attitude as compensation for insecurity.

4. A mild depression caused by isolation and the feelings of loneliness.

5. Introversion and increased sensitivity with querulous and paranoid attitudes.

6. A free-floating anxiety caused by death among the same age group.[12]

There are many avenues out of the world of loneliness. Many adults withdraw, especially after the death of a loved one. Others are able to make the adjustment and even broaden their interests and involvement as a means of compensating for their loss. In what way does the adult class meet their needs at this time? How can you as the teacher bring your teaching into their lives at this point?

Unmarried adults do not experience the loneliness that accompanies loss of a mate. They have learned long ago to fill their lives with other activities and interests to make up for the lack of companionship of a spouse.

Becoming a Part of the Older Adult Society ▪ Adults either accept older adulthood or reject it. Those who reject it have perhaps been influenced by our youth-oriented society. Older adults usually learn quickly that they are different from the younger group. They face fatigue and inadequacy if they attempt to keep up with young people. This does not mean that they should not be involved with all age groups. The isolation that occurs when one lives in a separated retirement center can be unhealthy. But the older adult does experience more of rigid age grouping. Most of his activities will be centered around those of similar age and interest.

During older adulthood a person's skills, vocational interests, abilities and avocational interests will be a basis upon which to build and continue friendships with people of the same age. A balance of study (older adults can still learn), recreation and service to others will meet needs and help the adult feel real satisfaction.

Social and Civic Activities ▪ Because of the number of older adults, the older adult exerts a significant amount of influence in public and political activities. They can still give political service and leadership. Their years of experience and training are an asset. Their involvement means they desire to keep pace with contemporary life and activities so their contributions have relevance.

In one church retired men supplement the ministerial staff. The church has hired several men for a dollar a year and they give 20 to 30 hours a week to the church. A retired businessman is the church business manager. A retired rancher is a minister of visitation to older adults. Another man skilled in electronics records and distributes tapes for the church. These men are considered to be a part of the church staff.

Many older adults could be given training classes at the church to learn how to minister in a new way to others. Perhaps some retired teachers could act as tutors after school for the youth and children. Those with other skills and abilities could teach classes to their own peer group or to other groups within or outside of the church.

The local church's Christian education program must be broad in order to minister sufficiently to this ever expanding group of adults. The activities and educational programs should be planned *with* and not for these people. The church can help the older adult find spiritual fulfillment. Feelings of uselessness, loneliness, depression and insecurity can be alleviated. Bible study and worship, social functions and recreational/educational outings, pastoral care and care or assistance in living conditions will be greatly appreciated and will draw older people to the church.

Educational facilities for the older adult should be carefully constructed with adequate lighting and microphone and hearing aid adapters if possible. Restrooms, no steps, skid-proof floor, adequate heating, easy access to transportation, electrical outlets placed higher to avoid having to stoop and an accessible church library will help meet their special needs.

A regularly functioning home department will extend the ministry of the church to those who cannot come to church.

Older adults are an integral part of the adult life of your church. Don't overlook them.

SOME QUESTIONS TO CONSIDER

1. How would you define the term adult?

2. What are the major characteristics of each of the three age levels of adults?

3. What implications does a knowledge of adult age level characteristics have for you as a teacher of adults?

FOOTNOTES

1. Paul B. Maves, *Understanding Ourselves As Adults* (Nashville: Abingdon Press, 1959), p. 15.
2. Adapted from Reuel L. Howe, *The Creative Years* (Greenwich, Conn.: Seabury Press, 1959), pp. 198-206.
3. Adapted from Douglas H. Heath, *Explorations of Maturity* (New York: Appleton-Century-Crofts, 1965), pp. 28-32.
4. Mervin B. Freedman, *The College Experience* (San Francisco: Jossey-Bass, 1967), pp. 27-31.
   Nevitt Sanford, *Self and Society* (New York: Atherton Press, 1966), pp. 52,274.
5. Clifford V. Anderson. "The Nature and Needs of Young Adults," *Adult Education in the Church* (Chicago: Moody Press, 1970).
6. From a lecture by Dr. Robert Shaper, Dean of Students at Fuller Theological Seminary, Pasadena, Calif.
7. Roy B. Zuck and Gene A. Getz, eds., *Adult Education in the Church* (Chicago: Moody Press, 1970).
8. Clifford B. Hicks, *Generation in the Middle* (Chicago: Blue Cross Association, 1970), p. 96.
9. Milton Leon Barron, *The Aging American* (New York: Crowell, 1961), pp. 239,240.
10. Ralph P. Beatty, *The Senior Citizen* (Springfield, Ill.: Charles C. Thomas, Publisher, 1962), p. 133.
11. Roy B. Zuck and Gene A. Getz, eds., *Adult Education in the Church* (Chicago: Moody Press, 1970), p. 61.
12. Kurt Wolff, *The Biological, Sociological and Psychological Aspects of Aging* (Springfield, Ill.: Charles C. Thomas, Publisher, 1959), p. 54.

Principles of Adult Learning

For over an hour eight-year-old Michael sat on the floor, listening to his mother explain the principles of skiing to her friend, Jean. He listened intently as she described the slipperiness of the icy slopes. He watched her demonstrate the binding release, the snowplow stance, and the kick-turn. He watched Jean practice "skiing" in the living room. Finally, he jumped up and begged, "Hey, Mom! Can I go skiing tomorrow with you guys? I learned while you were teaching Jean!"

But Jean hadn't *learned* to ski yet! She had gained some knowledge about *how to ski*, but the skill was still not acquired. That would take hours of actual practice on the slopes.

By the end of the next day, after six straight hours of work, Jean smiled happily at her accomplishment. "Oh I'm sore!" she groaned, "but that last time I only fell down once!" Jean had learned to ski—at least a little bit—on an easy slope. Each trip to the mountains since then has improved her skills until she now confidently manages even difficult runs.

WHAT IS LEARNING?

The most simple definition is that *learning is change*. Randolph Crump Miller said, "Learning occurs when a person responds to a situation of curiosity, relief of frustration, knowledge of facts or insight into the meaning of life. Behind the process is some kind of motivation, and out of it come various degrees of satisfaction."[1]

When we learn something, we make a change in our attitudes, ideas or actions. Often, more than one change occurs, for these three aspects of ourselves are interrelated. When my idea of a person changes, so do my attitudes and actions toward that person.

The ultimate goal in Christian education in the adult department of the church is for adults to move toward spiritual maturity as individuals.

In Christian education, therefore, learning is any change which moves the believer toward conformity with Jesus Christ, the ideal model of spiritual maturity (see Eph. 4:15).

Paul challenges us to change in Romans 12:1,2. "Therefore, my brothers, I implore you by God's mercy to offer your very selves to him: a living sacrifice, dedicated and fit for his acceptance, the worship offered by mind and heart. Adapt yourselves no longer to the pattern of this present world, but let your minds be remade and your whole nature thus transformed" (*NEB*).

Now, *that's* learning!

Is it reasonable to expect the adults in a Sunday School class to learn? Do the adults who come to your class learn the way Paul described in the above verses? How many adults come to class expecting to learn? If learning occurs, is it by accident or by design?

Yes, it is reasonable and biblical to expect our adults to learn, to change. You can help adults learn even if they do not come to the session expecting to learn. And while some learning may occur accidentally, you can so structure the session that planned learning will also occur.

Adults can and will change. One aspect of change is that it has some direction. Change can be an alteration of direction toward a wrong goal or a right one. Hopefully, in adult Christian education there will be change toward the proper goal. Perhaps the word "transformation" indicates the true meaning of change for the Christian. The Christian is to be totally transformed in both heart and mind. The Christian should be open to change of his total being.

Many people are satisfied with the acquisition of information but this is only the beginning of the learning process. When additional information has been gathered a person needs to ask himself these questions as suggested by Martha Leypoldt: "What has happened to me because I have this new information? How does this information assist me to help myself and others? What kind of person am I because I have this added information? Am I in the process of becoming a more effective Christian because of these insights? How is the Holy Spirit working in my life so that this information is making me more adequate for the tasks of today in this fast-changing world?"[2] That which a person adds to what he already knows may have the *least* impact upon him as an individual.

How a person feels about what he hears and reads is more important than the mere gaining of information. A person's emotional reaction toward information, ideas and facts may determine whether or not he learns.

What is the emphasis in your Sunday School class? Does the material that you present have personal meaning for your adult class members? What about Mr. Peterson who has been out of work for the last month? What about Mr. Jancy whose oldest son was killed in the war and his daughter is using drugs? What about Mrs. James who is worried about her physical health? What about Mrs. Lewis who attends church for the purpose of meeting new prospects for her real estate business? Does your Sunday School session cut through the barriers and penetrate to the personal lives and needs of these people?

Are your adults open to new ideas, methods of teaching or subjects? Are they willing to try something new or are they tied to tradition? How do you react when you are in a new situation or are presented with a new idea? Do you accept it? Do you like to be exposed to something new? Do you always feel positive? Do your students?

Negative feelings sometimes arise when new concepts and ideas are presented. Martha Leypoldt advises that when you feel resistance on the part of your adults you should stop and discuss these questions with them:

1. "Why do I keep my mind closed to new information? Is it because I feel insignificant that I close my mind when new situations confront me?

2. Am I reacting to a person or to preconceived prejudices rather than to the new idea or new information? Would the same information given by someone else or said in a different way make a difference in whether I accept it?

3. Am I allowing the Holy Spirit to work in me to help me in my attitudes toward others so that I may love more, be more patient, be more understanding, and therefore be more open to new insights into God's Word and His ways in my life?"[3]

One function of a teacher of adults is to help his class members perceive their own personal need to change. In other words, a teacher works to reveal a need for learning, then guides the adults in meeting that need.

DISTINCTIVES OF ADULT LEARNING

Although many facets of the teaching/learning process apply equally to children, youth and adults, there are some distinctive characteristics to adult learning. The adult teacher who is aware of these characteristics increases the opportunity for effectiveness in his teaching ministry.

1. Many of the adults that come to your class do not come with a *learner's attitude*. Many are accustomed to producing and working, but classroom students they are not! For most of the week they are involved in accomplishing, not in sitting back and learning. But whether they realize it or not they *are* learning! It may not be in an academic or structured setting such as a Sunday School class but they still learn. They note the trends in the stock market, changes in laws, hear of new methods of discipline or try

new recipes. In these settings the adult feels the need for special information and exerts the effort to obtain it. Does this happen in your Sunday School class? Do your students see themselves as being able to learn in your class? Do they feel that they can find information here that they need?

Of course, you will also have a significant number of adults who *do* know what it means to be students in an academic setting. It is estimated that each year one in every three adults in the United States participates in some kind of educational endeavor, and many engage in several each year! Since they do have these experiences, they have something with which to compare your educational techniques. These people will be expecting you to challenge *them* to produce and learn.

2. Many of your class members will come with *definite ideas*. In adulthood, personality and beliefs may be set and even rigid. Adults are somewhat resistant to change as this would upset the stability in their lives. But people will change if they see what is being offered in the class is related to their everyday lives and promises to make them more productive.

3. Your adults come to your class with much more experience than children or youth have. They have had a greater exposure to ideas and experiences. What does this mean for you as you plan to conduct your class session? The individuals in your room have much to contribute to the learning experience and they may feel thwarted if they are not allowed to participate and learn from one another as well as from you. And because of their background they are able to relate new information and experiences to their own lives more easily than the other age groups. A group of 12-15 adults will represent a greater variety of skills, experience, interests and education than a similar group of young people. Through individual conferences, interest finders and questionnaires, you will be able to determine the background and capabilities of your own class members. This information will assist you in preparing for your class Sunday by Sunday.

4. Another factor about the learning characteristics of adults has great importance. Adults are accustomed to the *immediate application of learning*. They do not want to wait. Bill is ready to try it "now." He asks, "How is this relevant to my life? Does this Bible lesson offer me anything now? I can't wait until next month. I have some needs and problems that must be satisfied now." Adults can also be pragmatic. They want to know if what you are teaching is really going to work in their lives.

The Bible study must give hope that what is being taught *will* make a difference. Use practical illustrations and examples from the lives of people like your class members to demonstrate the practicality of the lesson material.

5. Adult involvement in learning is *basically voluntary*. Compelling adults to participate in a program just because it is being offered only guarantees attendance, not learning! The needs of the adults and attractiveness of the course offered must be united. Adults want whatever they are being asked to learn to be directly related to their concerns and interests. They ask, "Why should I learn this? Why will knowing this be of value to me?" They may withdraw from a learning experience that does not satisfy them.

6. Adults have a tendency to be *apprehensive in learning situations*, and this affects the progress of the class and the individual. An adult who is apprehensive will not easily open up and share personal information or ask questions. Some adults are so uncomfortable in new situations that they avoid any organized groups, whether in social or classroom settings. They are afraid. This fear stems from many reasons. Many adults are fearful of revealing their ignorance. They are supposed to "know," especially the Bible, if they have been in church for many years. They inwardly hope that they will not be asked to share or defend what they believe. They want to feel responsible and in control at all times. Many of the problems the adult faces in daily life do not lend themselves to clear definite answers as far as he is concerned. He is somewhat intimidated by situations

in which his self-image is threatened. There is also a fear of being in a learning situation where disagreement may arise. It might cause him pain to differ with someone unless there is an open, accepting atmosphere. It is easier to remain a passive listener and let someone else speak with authority.

7. Adults *learn through their own efforts*. They can be guided, encouraged, excited and motivated by an outside force, but the learner himself must do the actual changing. This change occurs when he "does" something—discusses, thinks, debates, practices. He must "internalize" the material so that it becomes his own.

In many adult classes the learning that occurs involves only the *mind*. This can be important but the involvement of the mind by itself is not sufficient. The accumulation of facts without their application to everyday life quickly leads to disinterest and noninvolvement. Learning is more than the transmission of information. For an adult to learn he must be totally involved. This means that his mind or thinking process must be engaged and his emotions must be active. How a person feels about what he hears you say or sees you do will affect what takes place in his life. When your class members become totally involved in the learning process they become self-motivated. One may ask to talk with you after class, or may ask for books to read during the week. Another may ask for clarification of some Bible verses. He may even suggest that you touch on some new topic or give suggestions for some discussion topics. If he is totally involved you will notice it by his attitude and behavior.

In what way have your adults had the opportunity in the past month to learn through their own efforts? How often have they discussed or practiced the principles studied in the class? Have you asked the question, "What do you see yourself doing if you put this Scripture into practice today?" Have you ever asked class members to teach one of the sessions? There are many ways in which adults can learn through their own efforts.

Many adults even enjoy and want to have a voice in selecting some of the methods to be used for their own learning experiences. They want to participate in the development of the program. Many request to be involved in setting the goals and objectives for their own class. What are your objectives? In what way could your adults assist you in clarifying them?

8. Adults learn by their *identification with groups*. If a person has attached himself to a certain group of individuals he has done so for a specific reason. He likes to be with them or they have something to offer him. He enjoys learning with people with whom he feels at ease. Adults also learn through their own creative participation with others in small groups. The atmosphere and friendliness that you help to generate in the class will do much to insure that learning occurs.

9. Adults also learn from their *association with their teachers* by imitation or modeling. A teacher must be the kind of person he wants his learners to be. Recent research has indicated that when a person teaches one thing and models something else, the teaching is much less effective than if he practices what he teaches. Therefore, a teacher has a better opportunity of being a successful teacher if he exhibits the qualities he is attempting to teach his adults.

10. *Feedback* is very important for adults. Learners need an opportunity to find out how they are doing. Ask questions, give tests and provide other opportunities regularly for your adults to share what they have learned.

11. Every adult teacher is privileged to be able to rely on the *Holy Spirit* to help bring about change. Robert Boelke wrote, "The reality of the encounter between Jesus Christ and the learner is also due to the power of the Holy Spirit. Persons may structure situations so that there is study of the Scriptures, but the Holy Spirit alone may effect the learning. Through the Holy Spirit, learners come to reassess and change their understandings, attitudes, values and motives."[4]

12. Adults also come into a learning situation with more *pressures and responsibility* than children or adolescents. If

they come to a study program in the evening after a hard day's work, they are often fatigued. Timing, therefore, is important in planning an adult education program.

These are a few of the learning distinctives of adults. There are more but these will serve to indicate that adults are different from children and youth in their attitudes and approaches to learning.

HINDRANCES TO LEARNING

"Wow! Am I glad to get out of there!" Byron commented to Ralph as they both left a training session on the job.

"I know what you mean," Ralph agreed. "Four hours in a stuffy, smoke-filled room, trying to hear a speaker over the noise of lawnmowers and tree trimmers outside the window was a bit much! Did you get any notes?"

"You've got to be kidding!" Byron laughed ruefully. "Guess I'll have to read the book for myself!"

In many learning situations (especially in some church classes) conditions exist which have a detrimental effect upon learning. Anything that causes physical or mental discomfort, any situation that causes a person to lose his self-respect, or makes him feel that he is wasting time, is detrimental to learning.

Noise, bright light shining into the learners' faces, heat, cold, drafts, uncomfortable seating, posts in the line of vision, people who speak too softly or too loudly, poor acoustics—will be tolerated just so long. Your adults need a change in posture occasionally too. A later chapter in this book will discuss the physical learning environment.

Another condition close to physical discomfort is *boredom*. Boredom occurs when information is presented in a monotone, when students must listen to information they already know, when teachers use impersonal, passive language, use just one method of teaching, or read out of the quarterly or textbook.

Boredom has been defined as the gap between the energy level and the activity level. Adults who are using their energy to be actively involved in learning have closed the gap and ceased to be bored.

To detect mental distress in a class is difficult. What turns some people on turns others off. But generally, sameness, repetition, mannerisms, unsuitable illustrations—also, too many or too few of them—and lack of depth or too much depth in the teacher cause mental discomfort. Since good adult teaching requires much learner participation, the actions of fellow class members also causes distress. Does the teacher fail to put the brakes on the person who talks too much or prays too long? Do some speak too softly? Do others ask foolish questions or keep airing their pet theories or pointing to others' "dirty wash"?

Unless the teacher speaks privately with such problem learners the entire class is sure to suffer. To rebuke such persons openly will embarrass them (and the class). And unless you remove the causes of such hindrances some of your sheep are going to look for greener pastures.

An extremely important factor that contributes to an adult's negative response toward learning is *frustration*. Frustration occurs when a person is seeking to achieve a goal only to find his way blocked. When a teacher presents information in large blocks or so fast that an adult cannot absorb what is being presented, he becomes frustrated. A teacher who does not speak distinctly can cause frustration, especially if the learner is keenly interested in what is being taught. When the direction of the lessons or the goals of the learning experience are hidden, when textbooks are too obscure, when print is too small, or when the teacher refuses to answer questions, frustration is created. Another condition which produces frustration is when a teacher does not realize that some class members must proceed at a slower pace than others. Not everyone learns at the same rate of speed.

To make the learning experience more enjoyable, and thus more effective, the teacher should make every effort to eliminate hindrances. As much care must be taken at this point as in lesson preparation itself.

MOTIVATION FOR LEARNING

Motivation is an important factor in learning. Children and youth go to school because they must. If an adult comes to a Bible study class, for the most part he comes because he wants to. His motivation will increase if he is challenged during the class session. The more he participates and becomes involved, the greater the level of motivation and degree of learning.

Many factors affect the adults' level of motivation. Adults are not most effectively taught by the lecture method. They resist highly dogmatic authoritarian teachers. They are somewhat critical and want solid reasons before they accept facts. They are suspicious of "pat" answers because they realize that many experiences in life have no easy answer.

Several basic principles affect learning and motivation. These principles must be understood and applied if you expect your adults to learn.

First, people will accept and continue to do those things which are pleasant and satisfying to them. They will also avoid doing those things which prove to be annoying or do not give them satisfaction. If your class members experience some personal satisfaction from each class session in Sunday School, they will tend to keep attending your class.

The law of primacy states that first impressions are the most lasting. If a visitor comes to class and finds a warm response from you and others, a comfortable room setting, and stimulating teaching with practical content he will get a favorable impression and a positive attitude toward the class. Why not ask your adults what their impressions were the first time they came to your class? How do you feel when you go into a new situation? Ask your class what they think could be done to give every newcomer a satisfying experience.

The psychologist also says that the more an action is repeated the more quickly it becomes a part of the person's life. If you are teaching your class how to share their faith in Christ, the more they practice this in roleplaying or in actually witnessing the more this will become a regular part of their everyday life. If an individual begins to have a regular time of daily devotions this can become a part of his daily life. Do you give your adults the opportunity to practice what you have taught them? Have you done this on a regular basis? How do you plan to do this during the next month?

Negatively, any information, fact or skill that a person learns but fails to use is soon forgotten. If your class members immediately use what you have taught them their ability to retain it is increased greatly. But if they fail to use it they quickly lose it. Do you create opportunities for action so that your adults are able to use what you teach? In what way could you do this for your next session?

Finally, the law of intensity says that an experience that is vivid, dramatic, exciting is more likely to be remembered than a routine one. If you make your subject matter come alive through vivid examples, visual aids and personal involvement you are helping to insure that your adults learn.

One final principle about adult learning must be remembered. The greater the attraction a person has for a subject the greater the degree of learning. People who have a deep interest in a subject talk about it a great deal, read about it, become involved in it, and encourage others to participate in it. These people keep coming back for more experiences with the subject. *The stronger a person is attracted to a subject and desires to study it, the more obstacles he will overcome to study it and continue to study.*

What makes a subject of such importance that an individual will persevere in his desire to know more about it? There are several factors involved. Any subject that helps to meet a need in the life of a person will find a receptive student. But it must be presented in such a way that the person realizes his needs are being satisfied. Subject areas in which a person *does well* as he studies them have a tendency to become favorite subjects. Some subjects become popular because they are associated with friends or instructors whom the person likes or admires. Finally, if the person is relatively comfortable when he is studying this subject he will have added interest and desire to study it.[5]

What can you do to increase a learner's motivation for learning? Adults are looking for learning situations which allow them to think a little better of themselves, meet their needs, become more proficient in their daily lives and which help them master a subject.

Here are some ways in which you can help your learners develop positive attitudes toward your class:

1. Acknowledge the responses that adults make as attempts to learn. Let them know that these *attempts* are accepted whether they are correct or incorrect. For instance, say, "That's an interesting viewpoint, Bob. Would anyone else like to share an idea?" or "I appreciate your interest in the subject, Helen."

2. Present information in small enough steps so that the learners can follow and understand. Don't give too much information too fast.

3. Give the learners sufficient guidelines so they know what to expect from the class. Tell them what you will be studying, how long it will take, and any assignments you expect them to complete.

4. Any time a learner shows interest toward the subject matter encourage him (reinforce his behavior). Say, "You've spent a lot of time studying the point, haven't you, Bill? I appreciate that."

5. Be aware of what your adults already know about the subject and adjust the material by dropping repetitious content. You may want to give a test at the beginning of a unit of study to find out how much your adults know.

6. Relate new information to old and incorporate it into the experiences of your class members, letting them see the build-up in understanding that is occurring in the learning process.

7. Treat class members as individuals and let them know that they are welcome in the class session. Be friendly and interested in them.

8. Use many teaching methods and a variety of visual aids to involve all of the senses. Adults profit more from the use of visual aids than any other age group, probably because they have such an accumulated exposure to them. Television, posters, billboards, mailing pieces—a thousand and one impressions enter their minds during the course of a day.

9. Help the learners successfully apply the subject matter to their everyday lives. Plan strategies with them for practicing Christian principles. This helps the adult develop confidence in himself and in his teacher.

Perhaps the most important motivating force in the entire teaching/learning process is the *expectation* of the teacher. Learners—and all adults—tend to want to do what is expected of them. If the teacher sets goals, lets them know the aim of the session, gives assignments and expects class members to complete them, and in every way he can imagine conveys these expectations of accomplishment to his learners, adults will respond. Then, when the teacher encourages and praises the results, the ensuing satisfaction to the learner will motivate him to new efforts.

SOME QUESTIONS TO CONSIDER

1. Apply your last Sunday's lesson to the quote by Randolph Crump Miller on the first part of this chapter. Did all the things he mentioned take place?

2. Of the 12 distinctives of adult Christian education given, select four which in your own situation make the most sense.

3. On a scale of 1-12 rate your last class session as to motivation. A score of 10 to 12 is Excellent; 7 to 9 is Good; and 1-6 is "Time to renovate."

FOOTNOTES

1. Randolph Crump Miller, *Education for Christian Living* (Englewood Cliffs, N.J.: Prentice-Hall, 1956).
2. Martha M. Leypoldt, *40 Ways to Teach in Groups* (Valley Forge: Judson Press, 1967), pp. 17,18.
3. Ibid., p. 18.
4. Robert R. Boelke, *Theories of Learning in Christian Education* (Philadelphia: Westminster Press, 1962), p. 131.
5. Adapted from Robert F. Mager, *Developing Attitude Toward Learning* (Belmont, Calif.: Fearon Publishers, 1968), p. 12.

The Teacher and the Learning Process

The most important element in teaching is *you*, the teacher! Quality teaching is accomplished by a quality person. The methods, setting, visuals are all a part of the teaching/learning process. But the quality of the teacher is the most important element in the teaching/learning process.

In order to effect significant learning, the teacher must establish a personal relationship with his learners. He must be approachable, open, genuine and honest. Like the apostle Paul, the teacher must be able and willing to share himself with others. "[So strongly] drawn to you, we were joyfully willing not only to impart to you the good news from God but our own lives as well, because you had become dear to us" (1 Thess. 2:8, *MLB*). This personal sharing, involvement or contact with learners is what is meant by the personal approach to teaching.

When you teach you will be called upon to complete specific tasks that are a definite part of the teaching process.

1. You will be asked to *illustrate*. What you are teaching must be related to what those adults already know. Your content should begin at their level of knowledge and build upon it.

2. *Defining* is a part of the teaching process. Don't assume that your adults know what certain terms mean. Teaching involves

defining words, problems and situations in terms that are within the learners' experience and understanding.

3. Take the content of each lesson apart piece by piece, and *analyze* it before class so that you will be able to help your learners analyze it during class. This involves presenting the content in small enough portions so your adults can understand and accept it.

4. Another task of the teacher is that of *asking questions*. Ask meaningful and thought-provoking questions to make your adults think, react and discover.

5. On the other hand you will also be called upon to *respond* to questions your learners ask you. Someone has suggested that teaching is perhaps most effective when it is in response to questions asked by the class members.

6. *Listen!* Listen to your adults so that you will better understand their questions, doubts, problems, and viewpoints that may disagree with your own. A teacher who fails to listen and answers a question too quickly is violating Scripture. James 1:19 says, "Let every man be swift to hear, slow to speak" (*KJV*).

7. When you teach, *present different views* on specific subjects. Discuss the material from many angles. Look at the Scripture passages from different viewpoints in order to discover the true meaning.

8. Don't teach using just one method. Instead, be in the constant process of *adjusting methods*. Adapt your method, language and terminology to the ability and maturity of your class members. Variety which has a purpose and is related to your learners is important for effective teaching.

WHAT IS TEACHING?

Let's look at a couple of definitions. "Teaching, in its simplest sense, is the communication of experience. This experience may consist of facts, truths, doctrines, ideas, or ideals, or it may consist of the processes or skills of an art. It may be taught by the use of words, by signs, by objects, by actions, or by examples; but whatever the substance, the mode, or the aim of the teaching, the act itself, fundamentally considered, is always substantially the same: it is a communication of experience. It is painting in the mind of another the picture in one's own—the shaping of the thought and understanding to the comprehension of some truth which the teacher knows and wishes to communicate."[1]

Here is another: "We know God's Word only when we personally experience what it says. So our *teaching* must be geared to helping students *experience* God's truth, not just know information about it.

"In this sense, *teaching* the Bible is far more like 'teaching' drivers' training than 'teaching' multiplication tables or American history. The goal for which our *teaching* must be geared is that our students will grow in the ability to *live* God's Word. We can never be satisfied with mere mental mastery of Bible truth. We must always be concerned about experiencing it.

"It's easier now to see why 'teaching' Greek mythology and *teaching* the Bible are two totally different tasks. At best, we can only teach mythology as interesting stories, as information, or ideas, which may excite our curiosity but which will not have any important effect on our life.

"At best, we can only teach the Bible as God's revelation of reality, a reality that we are called as God's children to trust so completely that we rest the full weight of our lives on doing what God says and shows us. Bible stories, Bible doctrine, Bible history, are all to have a decisive impact on our lives!

"This is why we must differentiate between 'teaching' and *teaching*. For there is a kind of 'teaching' which is designed to communicate information, to tell stories. And there is *another* kind of *teaching* that is designed to have an impact on life."[2]

We believe that good adult Sunday School teaching consists of *providing* an atmosphere of openness and informality, *encouraging* learners to participate in the learning process, *leading* learners to the achievement of their goal of "living the Word," and modeling by the teacher of a life of openness and response to change.

THE LEARNING CYCLE

We strongly believe that the way teachers teach should be determined by the way learners learn. That may sound like an oversimplification, but there's a great deal of truth in that statement. If we do not understand the God-given process by which people learn our teaching may amount to no more than busy work—lots of teaching activity but little or no lasting change in the learners. Another way to say it is the teacher hasn't taught until the learner has learned.

But there is an orderly process by which people learn. We call the process the Learning Cycle. If the teacher ignores God's plan for learning, his teaching will be largely ineffective. But if the teacher cooperates with the learning process, he can expect consistent spiritual growth in the lives of those for whom he is responsible in the teaching ministry.

We see five distinct stages in the Learning Cycle—Approach, Explore, Discover, Appropriate, Assume Responsibility.

Approach

The Approach stage of the Learning Cycle is where curiosity and interest are aroused. At this point, something catches the learner's attention which draws him into the next stages of the process. A housewife sees a poster in the supermarket advertising a macramé class. She says to herself, "That sounds interesting. I'd like to learn to do macramé. I think I'll go sign up for that class."

In the Bible teaching ministry, the teacher must plan some ways to catch the interest of his class members and cause them to want to learn more about the session topic. For example, if your class session was from Matthew 5:21-26 (Jesus equating a hateful attitude with murder), you might arouse interest in the subject by provoking a discussion on manslaughter or justifiable homicide. Or you may simply ask the question, "When was the last time you murdered someone?" That will arouse interest and prepare learners for studying Matthew 5:21-26.

Explore

Once learners are interested in the subject at hand they are ready to explore the subject to answer the question, "What's it all about?" This is the fact-finding, information-gathering stage of the Learning Cycle. When the housewife attends her first macramé class session, she sees a beautiful macramé wall-hanging, feels various thicknesses of jute rope and hears the class leader explain that macramé is basically a technique of tying various knots in the jute to achieve the desired product.

In the Matthew 5:21-26 lesson, the teacher directs the class members to explore the passage by reading and paraphrasing the verses. One of the learners, Brian, summarizes his exploration by writing, "Jesus said that a Jew who calls his brother a good-for-nothing needs to apologize and ask forgiveness."

Discover

During the process of exploration, the learner eventually comes to a point of discovery. It's as if a light flashes on inside and he says, "I understand what this means!" The macramé student follows the directions in a macramé instruction booklet for tying a series of knots. Suddenly her eyes widen and she says, "I get it! I get it!" as she discovers how several knot combinations fit together to form a simple design.

As Brian and the other learners search through Matthew 5:21-26, the Holy Spirit does some illuminating too. As they discuss their paraphrases, Brian remarks, "And that means that any believer who harbors a hateful attitude toward another believer is guilty of murdering him in his heart." In the process of exploring what the passage says, Brian has discovered what the passage means to believers today.

Appropriate

Once a learner has been involved in exploration and discovery, he is ready to answer the question, "What does this mean to me?" In order to effect a change in his life, the learner must apply his general discovery to the specifics of his own life. The housewife soon realizes that she doesn't need to follow the patterns in the book any more. She has discovered enough about the various knots that she can begin to design a wall-hanging by creating her own pattern. She has begun to apply her basic knowledge of macramé to her needs for decoration in her own home.

Shortly after Brian had announced his discovery to three others sitting with him, the teacher asked each person to think of a relationship in which they harbored some hatred for another believer. The question hit Brian between the eyes; he immediately thought of a co-worker named Frank. Frank was from another church in town and really rubbed Brian the wrong way. Brian realized that his attitude toward Frank was wrong as he wrote on his worksheet, "I realize that my hateful attitude toward Frank is the same as murder in God's eyes."

Assume Responsibility

After a learner has explored the material at hand, discovered its meaning and applied his discovery to his own life, he must assume personal responsibility to change his behavior in light of what he has learned. Changed behavior is the culmination of the learning process and the proof that learning has taken place.

Our macramé artist designed and made a macramé wall-hanging with her own hands. It hangs in her den—and others like it now hang in the homes of her friends—as undeniable evidence that she has learned how to macramé.

Before the class session concluded, Brian asked God to help him change his attitude toward Frank. Before he left the classroom, Brian had decided on three ways by which he could begin to change his attitude toward Frank: pray for him daily (he wrote himself a note to tape to the bathroom mirror as a reminder); greet him warmly each day by saying something positive and affirmative; take him out to lunch in order to get to know him better.

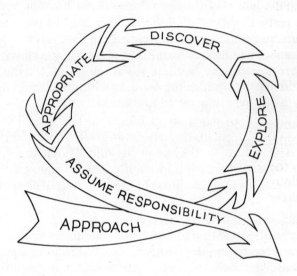

THE TEACHER'S ROLE

The Learning Cycle carries some implications for the teacher which must be understood. If the class members learn most effectively by being involved themselves in exploring, discovering, appropriating and assuming responsibility in the light of God's Word, what is the teacher's role? If the teacher is no longer primarily the dispenser of knowledge, what function does he serve?

The teacher has at least three vital roles to play in conjunction with the Learning Cycle: to guide adults through the cycle; to motivate them to learn; and to build positive relationships with his class members.

Guiding Adults

A guide is someone who knows the way to somewhere and who can show others how to get there. A teacher must be a good guide for his learners. He must know where he wants his adults to go in relation to the biblical principles they will study. And he must know *how* to lead them to that point.

First he must consider the individuals in his class and their special needs. Then he sets learning goals and plans classroom experiences to help the learners reach the goals. During the sessions the teacher guides the learners with much individual attention to discover new truths for themselves.

Jesus gives us an example to follow when being guides. "When he putteth forth his own sheep, he goeth before them, and the sheep follow him: for they know his voice" (John 10:4, *KJV*). A teacher who has already thoroughly learned the scriptural truths he wants his class members to apply in their lives can be a good guide.

When the teacher decides that it is better to be a guide, he may find it very difficult at first to make the transition from *one who tells* to *one who guides*. Most teachers use the teaching methods that were used by their own past teachers, and so they continue to perpetuate passive learning practices.

One way to make the transition easier is for a teacher to expose himself to effective involvement learning situations, as those provided at the International Center for Learning Seminars and Clinics. These seminars and clinics will not only provide opportunities for teachers to experience involvement learning, but also to plan (under the guidance of the seminar leaders) involvement learning for their adults.

Motivating Adults

A teacher must motivate his learners and make learning exciting and fun for them. He must raise questions to which his learners will want to find answers. He must learn how to guide them into learning through this method. He will have to plan to actively involve the learners in the session, and to use the classroom environment creatively.

To make learning exciting means teaching learners to explore and discover truths for themselves. Teachers who are afraid to let adults explore the Word of God for themselves deny the New Testament doctrine of the priesthood of the Holy Spirit to lead each adult to the true understanding of Scripture.

Relating to Adults

In order to teach effectively, a teacher must become involved with his class members on a personal level. When a teacher genuinely cares for his learners, he will be their friend and spend time with them. He will be available to them, not just on Sunday but also during the week.

Jesus did this. He had dinner at Matthew's house and at Zacchaeus' house and with the tax collector's sinner friends. When Peter's mother-in-law was ill Jesus visited in the home. He frequently accepted hospitality in the home of Mary, Martha and Lazarus. He went with His disciples to be where they were. He also took them with Him as He was going from place to place. They spent time with Him when He was teaching the multitudes and also when He withdrew alone to pray. They were with Him when He was transfigured and also when His spirit was distressed in Gethsemane. They learned from being with Him and by observing His behavior in the good times and the bad times.

ROLE OF THE HOLY SPIRIT

For teaching to result in genuine life changes both teachers and learners must give the Holy Spirit His rightful place in the process. We are seeking to teach and to learn spiritual truths, not just intellectual facts. We are also seeking changes in our attitudes and behavior which only come from strong inner motivation. The Holy Spirit is the only one who can motivate genuine and permanent life changes. "For God is at work within you, helping you want to obey him, and then helping you do what he wants" (Phil. 2:13, *TLB*).

SOME QUESTIONS TO CONSIDER

1. Write your own definition of "teaching."

2. Describe the five steps of the Learning Cycle in your own words.

3. Think of the teacher's role described in this chapter and list three ways you have been a good guide and an effective motivator in your teaching.

4. In what ways have you built positive relationships with and cared for your adults?

5. How does the Holy Spirit assist the teacher in preparing the session?

FOOTNOTES

1. John Milton Gregory, *The Seven Laws of Teaching* (Grand Rapids: Baker Book House, 1955), p. 2.

2. Lawrence O. Richards, *You—the Teacher* (Chicago: Moody Press, 1972), pp. 63,64.

Organizing for Learning and Growth

WHY ORGANIZE?

How many "fly-by-the-seat-of-the-pants" ventures have you seen which effectively accomplished anything over a long period of time? A business which is unorganized and poorly administered will likely go bankrupt in a short time. A married couple which does not develop some kind of strategy for finances, child rearing, communication, and responsibilities in the home will undoubtedly experience tension and disunity. Similarly, meaningful learning and growth in your adult Sunday School class will rarely happen without some plan of organization.

Organize to Involve

It should be remembered that organization is not an end in itself. It can be used, however, to better meet the needs of our learners. The first consideration in organizing adults is the need they have to most effectively be involved in the learning experiences which make up their Christian education. Learning is an active process; we all learn by doing. (Which is why correspondence courses in swimming have never been very successful!) A student must be encouraged to participate in, not just be a spectator of, the learning process. Maximum learning will not take place with minimum involvement, and this maximum involvement should extend beyond the classroom. Adults need to be actively involved with one another—in social activities, outreach efforts, and service projects associated with their Sunday School class. If they are, it will help meet the need for Christian fellowship. It will help each person feel that he is a participating member of the Body of Christ throughout the week as well as on Sunday. As a result of this continuing involvement outside of the classroom, relationships deepen and become more significant. Classroom interaction then becomes less superficial, and spiritual maturity is achieved more rapidly. So one of the first things to be considered is the importance of getting people deeply involved with the Word of God and with one another both in and outside of class.

Organize to Unify

The second consideration to keep in mind in organizing adults is the importance of establishing a group of the recommended size. Trying to secure maximum involvement in too large a group often does nothing but frustrate everyone. It proves cumbersome, inefficient, and doesn't produce the desired results. There must be a definite limit to class size, and this will be discussed a bit later.

ORGANIZATIONAL GUIDELINES

Providing for maximum involvement and establishing individual classes of a size so that they can function properly are the goals of our organizational efforts. There are guidelines to help achieve these two things.

Who Is an Adult?

In placing people together in an adult group, one of the first considerations is, "Who is an adult?" For the purposes of this book, an adult is a person who is 18 years of age or older. Today 18-year-olds are accepting adult responsibilities in many areas.

They have voting rights and an ever-increasing number of them are marrying and accepting the adult responsibilities of raising a family. Considering their role in our society, it is not inconsistent to categorize them as adults. But there are factors other than age which can serve as guidelines for grouping adults.

What Are His Needs?

The life needs which adults have must also be considered. These needs must be ministered to by relevantly applying the Word of God to adults' daily experiences. For example, scriptural principles of stewardship give guidelines for the use of time, money, and the abilities which God has given to each believer. Moreover, the Word of God speaks on the issue of parent-child relationships. And biblical directives are given concerning employer-employee relationships. In a real sense the Word of God was designed by the Holy Spirit to speak to man where he is—in need of wisdom, guidance, and direction for living on.a day-to-day basis. In this sense, adults are all in the same boat; there is a similarity of life needs among them.

WHY GROUP BY AGE?

There is a place to start the process of grouping adults. In most cases, whether the church is large or small, it has been found that one of the most effective ways of grouping adults is by their age. Here are the three primary reasons for doing so.

Similarity of Needs

First, there is a similarity of problems and needs among adults of the same general age level. To illustrate this, think of some individuals you know in their 30s. Isn't it true that they have similar interests with respect to marriage and family relationships, their stage of career development, and their physical health? Their interests in these three areas might be quite different from those held by people in the over-65 age bracket. Age grouping tends to cluster together people who have similar needs and interests. And this helps in making teaching more effective and social exchanges and interaction more compatible.

Easily Understood

The second advantage of age grouping is that it is easily understood by the participants. It is wonderfully inclusive. Everyone has an age and can therefore immediately determine in what group he belongs. There are only two possible difficulties that might be run into: (1) Some folks might not want to "fess up" to being a particular age, and (2) A married couple of different individual ages might find it difficult trying to decide which class to attend if they happened to find themselves "eligible" for two different age groups.

The second problem can be solved in one of two ways. Either the couple can choose which of the two groups they would rather be in or they can add up their two ages, divide by two, and take this average figure as the determining factor in deciding in which group they belong.

If a person is unwilling to "fess up" to his age, be sure he understands why he is being asked to attend a group of his own general age—to better meet the spiritual needs of all concerned. Appeal to his maturity and spirit of cooperation. If he is still unconvinced of the values of attending a particular class there is only one alternative: let him go where he will. It's better to have him in the "wrong" class than not in Sunday School at all!

Easily Developed and Administered

A third advantage of age grouping is that it makes it easy to develop and administer an adult department or division. It is a functional and workable way of dealing with the problem from the Sunday School administrator's standpoint and everybody is included, because each person has an age classification. Visitors are quickly and easily placed into the proper group. The size of classes can be administratively controlled by decreasing the size of the age span when the class should be divided to form two new learning units. It is uncomplicated, and everyone can understand it.

HOW BIG IS TOO BIG?

The position taken in this book is that the manageable size of an adult Sunday School class is 30 in attendance. The reasons for this number are given below.

30—a Manageable Number

1. *To promote a student-teacher relationship* ■ The first reason for suggesting that 30 is the recommended number for an adult class is because Sunday School is striving for educational soundness in its classrooms.

An important factor in the learning process is the student-teacher relationships. When Sunday School is discussed, one is talking about a teacher ministering to the needs of students. One is talking about developing disciples of Jesus Christ. This goes far beyond the mere impartation of knowledge. It means being open and honest and vulnerable—the sharing of a life. A familiar old poem expresses the importance of the student-teacher relationship.

> Mark Hopkins sat on one end of a log,
> A farm boy sat on the other.
> Mark Hopkins came as a pedagogue,
> And taught as an elder brother.
> I don't care what Mark Hopkins taught—
> If his Latin were crude and his Greek were naught.
> For the farmer's boy, he thought, thought he—
> All through lecture time and quiz—
> The kind of man I mean to be
> Is the kind of man Mark Hopkins is.

This poem helps to illustrate the fact that at any stage of

maturity the student-teacher relationship is an important one. Limiting a class to 30 in number helps encourage a meaningful relationship between the teacher and the students.

2. **To promote group interaction** ▪ Person-to-person interaction is encouraged in a smaller group, and this is the second reason for maintaining 30 as a workable size for a Sunday School class. Sharing solutions to common problems can be a helpful thing in our classes. People are much more apt to share in a group of 30 than they are in a group of 60 or 90 or more.

People rarely interact with more than 30 others (if that many) in any given social activity. We gather and converse in relatively small groups. Yet 30 is a large enough number to insure everyone having fellowship. From a standpoint of the small number of people we relate to and converse with in a social situation, there isn't any need for having classes larger than 30.

3. **To create a greater teaching variety.** ▪ Teaching methods such as buzz groups, discussion, and circle response can best be managed in the relatively small group of 30 in number. This size is a great help in promoting a greater variety of teaching methods and devices.

4. **To promote leadership.** ▪ The fourth reason for limiting adult class sizes to 30 is to provide sufficient leadership for future growth and outreach. If a large class of 90 is divided into three classes of 30 each, three times as many teachers will be needed. With leadership at a premium in most churches, it may seem as if this is defeating the purpose by creating the need for additional class officers and teachers. But smaller class size makes the recruitment of teachers and leaders easier. Many people who may feel unqualified to teach a group of 90 or 100 might "give it a try" with a smaller group. In this way, leadership is allowed to emerge; consequently, it is possible to have more leaders recruited, trained, and developed.

5. *To facilitate administration.* ■ Fifth, this size of 30 takes into account the administration concept of a ratio of five-to-one of followers to leader. This concept will be discussed below and explained further. But a class size of 30 allows the class to be divided into workable units of follow-up, outreach, and social activity.

Span of Control

Picture in your mind's eye a typical organizational chart. It looks something like this:

SPAN OF CONTROL CHART

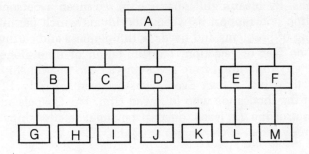

Notice that person "B" has 2 people ("G" and "H") who are responsible to him and for whom he is responsible. Persons "E" and "F" each have 1 ("L" and "M," respectively). Person "D" has 3 people ("I," "J," and "K") who, in a sense work for him. Person "A" has the largest number in his staff (persons "B" through "F").

Look at the chart again. Person "B" has 2 people reporting to him—or a "span of control" of 2. Persons "E" and "F" each have a span of control of 1. How large is person "D's" span of control? (If you said 3, you're right! Keep this up and you'll graduate with honors!) Person "A" has a span of control of 5. Persons "A," "B,"

"D," "E," and "F" administratively (not *dictatorially*) control the people directly below them on the chart. All that this means is that the responsibility for the operation of the organization has been divided up and delegated to other people. If a problem arises in person "L's" department, chief executive "A" simply talks to person "E" and helps him solve the problem. So it can be seen that span of control simply refers to the number of individuals reporting or responsible to any one leader or officer.

From the standpoint of organizational efficiency, no one person should have more than five or six people directly responsible to him.

Furthermore, the experts tell us that it is impossible to maintain a meaningful relationship with more than about seven persons. By meaningful relationship we mean a personal interaction and rapport between individuals which permits the sharing of problems and needs with openness and caring, and with no fear or rejection. The limitation of time alone prohibits any individual from achieving a deep relationship with more than just a few. Even Jesus focused on only 12 men out of the thousands who followed Him. The Gospels suggest that out of the 12, Jesus' deepest personal relationships were with only three—Peter, James and John.

Class Units

The entire class should recognize its responsibility for contacting prospective class members. This outreach can be made more effective by organizing and administering the efforts of the class as a whole. The responsibility for coordinating the class's outreach efforts should be delegated to an individual. The logical person to fill this role would be the class president. To emphasize his leadership role, it would be well to designate his title as that of "class leader"—one of his major responsibilities being to lead and coordinate the entire class in contacting prospects.

One of the most efficient ways for him to do this would be to divide the class into groups or units. Remembering the span of control ratio of 5- or 6-to-1, the class of 30 is best divided up into 5 units. This would result in the 5 units having about 6 members each. (Or this could be 6 couples, which would give even fewer units. The unit leaders would have greater responsibility, the class leader less. It might be more efficient this way.)

We suggest that these class units be called caring units and that their functions include interaction and growth beyond the classroom. Chapter 12 details the ministry of caring which can result from the caring unit approach in your church.

Since it is best for the class leader to have only 5 or 6 people and not 30 people reporting to him, it is clear that each of the 5 units would need to have one of its members function as the unit leader. The person filling this role would have the other 5 or 6 members responsible to him. So, limiting the class size to 30 in number allows us to organize the class's outreach efforts utilizing the span of control ratio of 5- or 6-to-1 on all levels.

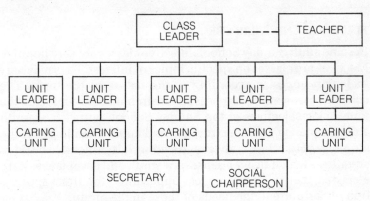

Maximum Class Size

It has been stated that the recommended class size is 30. What happens when our outreach efforts prove effective and new people join our class? How do we handle this numerical growth? Is there a maximum size to which we should limit our classes? Yes, there is. When the class reaches 40 in attendance, it is time to create a new learning unit. The group of 40 should be divided into two groups of 20 each. When these two new groups each reach 40, they should in turn divide into two groups of 20 each. It is surprising how rapidly numerical growth can take place with everyone doing his part in the matter of outreach.

How Small Is Too Small?

It should be recognized that for many churches, classes of 30 in number are in the future. Rather than maximum size, they may be struggling with the question of minimum size. Can one have an effective class with just 1 or 2 people in it? Most certainly the process of discipleship can work on a one-to-one basis. But as a general rule, the minimum effective number for an adult class would be 5 members. The learners plus the teacher would form one outreach unit themselves, and motivation for growth would be high. Less than that number often tends to be discouraging.

ELECTIVES AND THEIR USE

In some adult Sunday Schools, elective classes are very popular. Electives are classes on specific topics of interest. They may vary in length and size according to the nature of the topic. The constant use of electives poses some hindrances to achieving the four major objectives of the Sunday School: outreach, warmth and acceptance, Bible instruction, and application to life. If the structure of the class is always changing, it is difficult to build in situations which foster a sense of warmth and acceptance. With electives, there may also be less opportunity for direct application of Scripture to the needs of those in the group.

A possible way to handle this when electives are used regularly is to see that everyone has a "home base," a group where he would be with others of his own age group. Then he could have his needs for continuing fellowship and accountability met. The following paragraphs and accompanying diagrams show three possible ways of handling the electives, while still achieving all four objectives of the Sunday School. Each plan begins with four "home base" classes of 30 adults each.

ELECTIVE PLAN 1

Offer one optional elective. A small number of people from each of the other permanent classes could choose to attend the elective for a limited period of time.

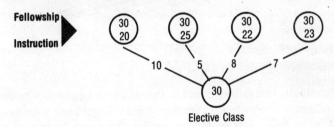

ELECTIVE PLAN 2

For three quarters of the year, everyone attends his regular classes based on age grouping. Then during the fourth quarter (perhaps summer) everyone attends the elective of his choice. Each class session begins with a time of fellowship in the regular classes, before everyone moves to his elective.

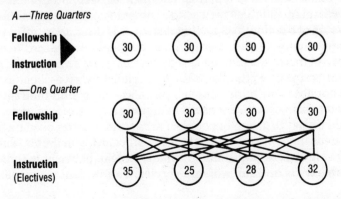

ELECTIVE PLAN 3

Have electives all year around. Allow everyone opportunity for a time of fellowship in his permanent class. Then the classes divide into electives for the instruction part of the class session.

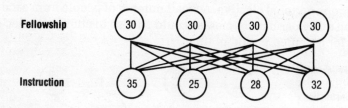

Fellowship   30   30   30   30

Instruction   35   25   28   32

THIS ORGANIZATION PLAN IS FLEXIBLE

The "limit-divide-grow" concept that is being suggested in this book will work whether a Sunday School is utilizing a uniform lesson plan (all adult classes studying the same lesson materials), an individual class lesson plan (each class studying a lesson which differs from that studied by other classes), or an elective class plan (entire classes or individuals within classes choosing a particular course of study from several different ones being offered simultaneously).

If plan 3 (an elective class plan) is used, the class in which a particular student is a permanent member becomes the "home base" out of which he may go to another location for class study time. When using this elective system, it is often more effective to have the class study period first and then move to the "home base" classes for a closing assembly time. Here's why:

1. By meeting after the teaching period, the last association a person has is with his "home base" class. He would then leave Sunday School with a sense of belonging and a sense of identity with a specific group of people. Perhaps he is better acquainted with these people than he is with any other group in the church.

2. The fellowship time allows for a break between the class study period and the worship service. The student would then

be better prepared for a more meaningful worship experience.

3. New people are more easily integrated into the home base class. They come back after the study time, which means that the unit leaders don't have to search frantically for the visitors who have scattered to the elective classes.

Group Your Adults

The best place to start is by placing the adults into three groups: Young Adults (18 to 35), Middle-aged Adults (36 to 59), and Older Adults (60 and above).

However, collegians seem to have unique characteristics and needs. For this reason, it is advantageous to have a separate class for them. Single adults are also helped by having a separate class—age grouped, of course, if there are that many.

Probably the easiest way to do this is to take an anonymous "age poll" of your adults. It can be as simple as passing out a three-by-five card to each person on which he is to put his age and marital status. These cards should be collected and kept as a source of age distribution information which can be used in establishing the number of classes.

Analyze Age Distribution ▪ The second step is to analyze the age distribution within each of these three large age groupings. They will need to be divided further because, ideally, there should not be a wider age span than 10 to 15 years in any group of adults. If this principle must be bent, however, it is most easily bent in the over-60 age bracket.

Thus in a group of adults aged 18 and older, you might wish to incorporate these age groupings: 18 to 24 (college age), 25 to 35, 36 to 49, 50 to 59, and 60 and above.

Separate by Age ▪ Now let's put it all together and see how this will work in actual practice. Let's assume for the purpose of illustration that there is an adult division in a Sunday School and it is comprised of 100 individuals.

Step 1: Gather the age distribution cards. After they are collated, the following age distribution has been arrived at: 33 people are Young Adults (age 18 to 35); there are 59 Middle-aged Adults (age 36 to 59); and there are 8 Older Adults (age 60 and above).

Step 2: Analyze the distribution within each of these larger age distributions. In so doing, it is discovered that 9 of the Young Adults are college age and 24 are not. Of these 24, 7 are single. Because of the unique needs of collegians and singles, it is best to have a separate class for each of them. Thus, there would be three Young Adult classes: 9 pupils in a college age class, 7 in a singles class, and 17 in a young marrieds class (a woman may attend Sunday School without her husband, or one partner may be teaching in another age group).

The analysis of the Middle-aged Adults reveals that of the total number of 59, 25 are in the 36 to 39 bracket, 15 are in the 40 to 49 bracket, and 19 people are in the 50 to 59 age division. This leaves 8 individuals in the 60 and above bracket.

Create Adult Classes ▪ Thus, with 100 individuals distributed as above, we would have 7 adult classes grouped in the following manner:

Young Adults	
College Age	9
Singles (25-35)	7
Marrieds (18-35)	17
Middle Adults	
Age 36 to 39	25
Age 40 to 49	15
Age 50 to 59	19
Older Adults	
Age 60 and over	8
Total	100

DON'T BE AFRAID!

Sometimes the discussion of organization is threatening to people because they immediately see themselves wrapped up in hours of paper work and administrative red tape. "I'll be glad to teach a class," they say, "but I don't have time to organize an entire Sunday School!"

We hope that you see the organizational principles presented in this chapter are designed to save you time and effort in administering your adult class—even when it grows to twice its present size. As you keep in mind the concepts of span of control, age grouping, and class size, you will find your task of teaching and leading to be more fruitful and of greater value to your individual learners.

SOME QUESTIONS TO CONSIDER

1. What are some good reasons for giving attention to organization in the adult Sunday School?

2. Why is it advantageous to group adults by age levels? What exceptions might there be for grouping them otherwise?

3. What is the ideal size for an adult class? What is the advantage of using this number as a guideline?

Leading Adults

"What a coincidence that you should ask me this morning if I would consider being a teacher in the Sunday School!" Walt laughed. "All week long God has been speaking to me about becoming more active in the church."

"It's no coincidence," Jack argued seriously. "Last Tuesday at our adult division planning meeting your name was brought up, along with three other names, as possible teachers for the new class. Right then we prayed together that God would guide our choice by preparing the heart of the one person He wanted to serve with us. Not one of the other three people were prepared. Yet, you've said that God has been speaking to you. Are you willing to share with me what you said back to Him?"

"Well, I asked Him to show me what He wanted me to do. Looks as if I'm going to be an adult Bible study teacher," Walt answered with a broad grin.

"Thank you for being open to God's leading, Walt. I am sure that as God's choice for the job you will be a great addition to our staff. We thought of you because you seem to have the qualifications we believe are necessary for being an effective teacher.

"Welcome aboard!"

QUALIFICATIONS OF A LEADER
IN THE ADULT SUNDAY SCHOOL

Many elements are involved in the learning process. Creative and appropriate methods are important. Total session teaching is valuable. Setting a learning environment is beneficial. Organizing and grouping effectively are worthwhile. But having the right leaders is essential.

What makes a good leader? What qualifications do you look for in a person you are considering for a position in your adult Sunday School? You will want to develop your own list of requirements which will meet the needs of your specific church. But we have found that the successful leaders in most Sunday Schools usually have the following characteristics in common.

1. He Is God's Choice for the Position.

God has always selected His leaders very carefully. Only He knows all of the requirements of every job and all of the unanticipated problems which will arise. And only He knows which person will best be able to handle the job. Yet, sometimes when God selects as a leader someone who seems to us unlikely to succeed, we need to be reminded of His wisdom. As God told Samuel, "I don't make decisions the way you do! Men judge by outward appearance, but I look at a man's thoughts and intentions" (1 Sam. 16:7, *TLB*).

When we do not let God select our leaders, we may select the wrong person. For example, not everyone should be a leader. "Not many of you should become teachers, my brothers, for you know that we (who teach) are assuming the more accountability" (Jas. 3:1, *MLB*). In the Scriptures we find several references to teachers who shouldn't have been teaching. Acts 15:24 records the account of some who attempted to turn Christianity into another kind of Judaism. There were teachers who attempted to teach others before they were grounded in the faith themselves (1 Tim. 1:6,7). Romans 2:17-23 contains the report of teachers who taught others and yet their own lives were a contradiction of their instructions. They did not live out the truth that they were teaching.

On the other hand, when you let God choose your leaders, He will bring you someone who will have all of the other qualifications!

2. He Has a Personal Relationship with God.

The leader of an adult Sunday School class must be committed to the claims of Christ and to God. He must have accepted Jesus Christ into his life and have turned his life over to the leading of the Holy Spirit. This leader realizes that, like the apostle Paul, he has been called to serve and rejoices to be a channel of God's love. "How thankful I am to Christ Jesus our Lord for choosing me as one of his messengers, and giving me the strength to be faithful to him" (1 Tim. 1:12, *TLB*). When a leader relies on the Lord's strength to be faithful, he won't forget to credit the Lord for his successes. Peter says that a successful leader is humble (1 Pet. 5:4,6). A committed leader will have the Word of God firmly implanted in his heart. He will "know what his Word says and means" (2 Tim. 2:15, *TLB*). His study of the Word will not be limited to studying for class. He may be in another Bible study class as a learner during the week, so that he can continue to grow.

3. He Is Ready to Lead.

You will want as a leader someone who is in a good place in their personal and spiritual growth from which to share. People who are living victoriously in spite of their day-to-day problems make exciting leaders and models. These people are prepared to lead because they are in regular communication with God. Their prayer lives include praying for others as well as for themselves. On the other hand someone who is really struggling in his spiritual life may not be ready to lead.

You will want a leader who lives what he teaches. Paul said he and his fellow workers lived as they did "in order to offer ourselves as a model for you, that you might follow our example" (2 Thess. 3:9). The leader makes a commitment to the lives of his learners. It is a commitment to be an example as well as a communicator of God's truth. If the leader wants his learners' lives to make a positive impact on their world, the leader must ask himself what kind of impact he is making in his world of everyday opportunities and responsibilities. The leader cannot ask or expect his learners to live beyond what he is committed to himself.

You will want a leader who understands the principles and processes of adult learning.

4. He Can Relate Well to Other Adults.

The leader's view of people, and especially his class members and fellow workers, must be one of respect for their ideas, attitudes, strengths and weaknesses. A leader will have to be patient with others who may not learn as quickly as he might wish they would. He should be able to listen attentively as people share their problems and ideas—some of which may be opposite to his own ideas. He will also have to be a person able to keep the confidences he hears absolutely confidential.

Basically, a good leader has learned the skills of building close, personal relationships with others.

WHO ARE THE LEADERS?

The responsibility of conducting an effective adult Sunday School is not the sole responsibility of the general superintendent or the teacher. Instead the responsibilities and tasks are shared by all of the leaders of the Sunday School. These leaders are the teacher, class leader, caring unit leaders, class secretary and social chairperson. In larger churches these may also be a department leader and even a division coordinator in the adult department.

Each leader has his own set of responsibilities as a part of the total operation of the Sunday School. Each member also has a responsibility to be cooperative and supportive to the other leaders so that they will function together toward the same goal.

The organizational relationships of the class leaders are shown on the following chart:

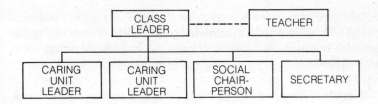

Teacher

"When I was first approached about becoming an adult teacher I thought you just wanted me to prepare and present a lesson each week," Virginia shared with her pastor one day. "Now look at me! Today I'm decorating for a class banquet. Yesterday I drove Mrs. Peters to the airport because she needed a ride. And last week I baby-sat two dogs and a cat for one of my class members who was going on vacation! Of course, I love every minute of it, but it seems to me that a teacher is many things!" she finished laughingly.

As a teacher what then is your task? What are you supposed to do? What is your role?

One of the finest descriptions of a teacher is stated by Dr. Earl V. Pullias and James D. Young in their book, *A Teacher Is Many Things*. They suggest that a teacher is "...a guide, a teacher, a modernizer: a bridge between generations, a model: an example, a searcher: one who does not know, a counselor: a confidante and friend, a creator: a stimulator of creativity, an authority: one who knows, an inspirer of vision, a doer of routine, a breaker of camp, a storyteller, an actor, a scene designer, a builder of community, a learner, a facer of reality, an emancipator, an evaluator, a conserver: one who redeems or saves, a culminator, a person."[1]

That's a large order for any one person. And yet at different times you will find yourself in each of these roles or will be called upon to exhibit these qualities. The Holy Spirit and Jesus Christ (who is "renewing the mind of the believer") are at work within you as you work with your students. Do not try to teach out of your own wisdom, knowledge or skill. You can claim the promise in Jeremiah 33:3: "Call unto me, and I will answer thee, and shew thee great and mighty things, which thou knowest not" (KJV).

Every teacher needs a class small enough so that he can teach and cultivate each learner spiritually. Bible study and learning methods are more effective in the small-class group because teacher and learners can interact more. The small-class group also makes it easier for the teacher to sustain attention and interest in the session and activities.

The following list of duties further defines the teacher's important role:

1. Guiding his class group in a life-related study of God's Word.

2. Guiding Bible learning methods for active and meaningful research and expression of study projects.

3. Cultivating the friendship and interests of learners and their families.

4. Leading learners into a progressive understanding of spiritual awareness and experience with Jesus Christ and His church.

5. Cooperating with other teachers in an outreach ministry.

6. Engaging in class and individual study opportunities that will improve his effectiveness.

7. Taking advantage of opportunities to improve his teaching.

8. Conducting planning meetings with the class leaders.

Secretary

"I really enjoy being a class secretary," Lewis shared one Sunday. "I feel it's really important that each guest be warmly greeted as he enters our classroom. And because I keep the records, I can often remember the names of our guests, and greet them by name when they return a second time. As I see it, this is my way of helping create a caring atmosphere in our class."

Here is a list of the secretary's duties:

1. Working in cooperation with the general Sunday School secretary to maintain the records system.

2. Maintaining the records system with accuracy.

3. Warmly greeting and welcoming learners from his desk near the entrance to the room.

4. Receiving, recording, reporting and submitting offerings to the general Sunday School secretary.

5. Studying and analyzing the records, reporting any information that will help improve the Sunday School ministry.

6. Assisting in preparing absentee follow-up information and/or materials for the teachers.

7. Attending and participating in the planning meetings.

Class Leader

Although the role of the adult class leader encompasses that of the traditional class president, it also goes beyond that.

1. The class leader is the primary administrator of the class. Under his direction the class does its part in achieving the four objectives of the Sunday School.

2. He helps to keep the class "people-oriented" by working closely with the unit leaders in contacting and cultivating prospective class members.

3. He shares planning responsibilities with the teacher for coordinating the entire class session.

4. He is the primary channel of communication between the Sunday School's administrative staff and the individual class.

5. As class administrator, he interprets the job descriptions for the other class leaders and helps them fulfill their duties.

Caring Unit Leader

The adult caring unit leader is an important position.

1. A unit leader functions as sort of an undershepherd. The members of his unit are his flock. This concept should be clarified. The unit leader is not in competition with the pastor.

The terms "undershepherd" and "flock" when applied to the unit leader refer to attitude, not office. He gets to know his unit members personally and is sensitive to their physical and spiritual needs.

The pastor should feel a sense of relief in knowing that there are other people who have genuine concern for members in the adult Sunday School classes. And as the unit leader ministers to his unit members, he should be sensitive to problems needing pastoral care. When he becomes aware of such problems, he should quickly alert the pastor concerning these needs.

2. The unit leader functions as a channel of communication, motivation and activation between the class leader and the unit members. The class leader looks to him to involve his unit members in class service projects and social activities.

3. When a new person begins attending the Sunday School class, he is placed into a unit by the class secretary. The unit leader welcomes the new member and helps him feel comfortable in the group. He makes sure the newcomer is introduced to the other unit members, as well as to the other class members. At class social functions the unit leader makes sure that any newcomers to his unit are integrated into the larger group.

4. On Sunday mornings and at out-of-class activities the unit leader makes a mental note of who in his unit is absent. He then contacts these absentees and expresses his love and concern for them. He is vital in making people feel wanted and accepted in the group.

Social Chairperson

The adult class social chairperson also has an important role to fulfill:

1. The social chairperson, who is directly responsible to the class leader, provides the leadership in planning social activities for the entire class. These social activities should take place on a regular basis—perhaps monthly.

The chairperson provides the leadership in planning, but he

doesn't do all the work! He should delegate much of the responsibility to other class members. In this way each class member has a ministry to the rest of the class, and each class member plays an important role in helping to achieve the four objectives of the adult Sunday School.

2. One of the reasons for limiting the size of an adult class is to assure maximum involvement of the members for both in-class and out-of-class activities. The social chairperson should give each person an opportunity to be actively involved in the social functions. The class social times should be structured so that members and visitors have the opportunity to get to know one another. Class socials should be a time of deepening interpersonal relationships.

As you can see each leader has a vital role to fill if the Sunday School is to reach its objectives.

ADDITIONAL LEADERS

Two more job descriptions are included for larger Sunday Schools. They describe the responsibilities of the department leader and division coordinator.

Department Leader

The department leader can help teachers and secretaries most effectively by encouraging them and assuring them of his support in their ministry. He should be alert to the way the entire Sunday morning program is being conducted. He should express appreciation for jobs well done so that teachers will have a sense of satisfaction in their work. He should give constructive suggestions, tactfully, to his teachers. The department leader needs to encourage teachers to try new, well-planned techniques that will help them achieve a greater measure of success. He also needs to listen attentively to teachers' suggestions and complaints. He should attempt to implement constructive ideas.

In addition to this continual process of supervision and guidance, the leader should participate with teachers in training classes, conventions, workshops and individual study. Listed below are the department leader's general duties:

1. Discovering, recommending and enlisting personnel for the Sunday School department as he works within the framework of the church policy.

2. Helping department teachers and officers to fulfill their assignments.

3. Functioning as the channel of communication between the Sunday School general superintendent, or division coordinator, and teachers and secretaries.

4. Representing the adult department at Sunday School planning meetings.

5. Evaluating the space and equipment of the department and recommending needs to the general superintendent.

6. Building the proper ratio of teacher to learners by creating needed classes as growth occurs.

7. Leading in a program of outreach in order to find those in the community who are not enlisted in Sunday School.

8. Seeking to develop and maintain a plan in which the teachers effectively enlist the cooperation of the families of their learners in deepening the impact of the Sunday School's education ministry.

The Division Coordinator

The division coordinator is responsible to the general superintendent for all of the above functions within his division. The coordinator needs to be knowledgeable in Christian education and he should work closely with the department leaders. He is personally involved in discovering, enlisting and training new staff members.

The division coordinator should have a deep concern for the Christian education of learners in the Sunday School and a keen awareness of how to make teaching/learning effective. This key position should be filled by a person of administrative ability, capable of guiding other people in their work. The coordinator's proper delegation of duties among his staff leaders is vital to his success.

The specific duties of the Sunday School division coordinator include:

1. Working within the framework of the church policy in discovering, recommending and enlisting personnel for the entire division.

2. Guiding department leaders in directing their teachers and secretaries in effective Sunday School ministry.

3. Functioning as the primary channel of communication between the Sunday School administration and the department leaders.

4. Representing the division at the Sunday School planning meetings.

5. Evaluating the space and equipment in the division and recommending needs to the general superintendent.

6. Developing and maintaining departments and classes of the proper size and teacher-pupil ratio by creating new departments and classes as growth occurs.

7. Guiding department leaders in a program of outreach in the community.

8. Meeting monthly with the department leaders for evaluation and planning.

9. Providing opportunities for training of prospective and present teachers and officers.

WHAT A JOB!

We can summarize by saying that effective Sunday School leaders are those whose personal lives are examples, whose relationship with God, and whose understanding of the Scriptures and the needs of their learners are such that the Holy Spirit can work in and through them and the learners to develop in each the desired spiritual maturity.

SOME QUESTIONS TO CONSIDER

1. List the basic qualifications for leaders given in this chapter.

2. Compare the job descriptions discussed to those used in your Sunday School. In what ways are they similar? Different?

3. What leaders might you add to your Sunday School to increase its effectiveness?

4. What organization changes might you make in your Sunday School to better minister to your adults?

FOOTNOTE

1. Earl V. Pullias and James D. Young, *A Teacher Is Many Things* (Bloomington, Indiana: Indiana University Press, 1969), p. VIII.

PART 2
ORGANIZING FOR LEARNING

An adult Sunday School has many individual elements.
These elements include grouping adults, the teaching
team, the time allowed, total session teaching, learning
objectives, session planning and the classroom environment. Each of these interrelated elements is essential
to the successful operation of the Sunday School. ▪ Part
Two of this book offers a discussion of each of the above
elements and gives standards which have proven successful in hundreds of adult Sunday Schools across
North America. ▪ It takes hours of planning, lots of
work and total cooperation from all of the leaders. But it
is worth the effort. Your adult Sunday School can run
like clockwork under the united direction of a dedicated teaching team.

Planning the Session

"What are you doing, Dad?" 13-year-old Kevin asked one Sunday afternoon.

"Preparing next Sunday's session for my adult class," his father answered.

"I thought you did that on Saturday nights after the movie on TV!" Kevin said with a puzzled look on his face.

"I know!" his dad replied with a smile. "And my class suffered from my shoddy planning. But I've come to realize how important it is to carefully and prayerfully prepare each session. I've been a better teacher—and it's made a tremendous difference in my class."

Many teachers feel the need for better preparation and admit that a more disciplined approach to preparation would benefit them as teachers and improve the effectiveness of their classes. But they don't know where to start. They seldom have a plan to guide them in preparation.

The following four-step plan is a logical, easy-to-follow approach to lesson preparation. It will be a helpful tool whether you're using fully prepared curriculum, study guide or the Bible alone.

1. STUDY, PRAY AND APPLY

The first step in planning the session is for you to get in touch with the session Scripture yourself. Spend plenty of time reading the Scripture from different versions and paraphrases. Keep a Bible dictionary and commentary handy for reference. Write

your own paraphrase of the Bible verses. It will help you evaluate your own understanding of the section. It is also helpful to
write out these three questions and your answers to them for the
passage you're studying: "What does the Bible say? What does it
mean? What does it mean to me?" The more study activity you
participate in during your preparation, the better equipped you
will be to guide the learning session for others.

Bathe your study time with prayer, asking the Holy Spirit for
insights into the Scripture passage. Remember, He is your partner in the teaching/learning task.

2. SELECT THE CENTRAL TRUTH FOR THE SESSION

As you study, look for one key point that applies to you and to
your class members. This will allow you to deal thoroughly with
one important issue during the class session, instead of hopping
from one minor point to another or thinking you are responsible
to tell everything you know about a passage.

In any given section of Scripture there may be several "central
truths"—key thoughts which could be the basis for a lesson. But
for effective teaching, you must narrow down your selection to
one point—and then stick to that point as you write learning
objectives and activities.

If you are using prepared curriculum, look for the central truth
which the editors have selected for the session. Carefully evaluate the central truth they have chosen in light of the needs of
your class members. If necessary, adapt the central truth to fit
your situation. Once you have isolated the central truth, write it
down and evaluate each succeeding planning step by it.

3. WRITE LEARNING OBJECTIVES FOR YOUR CLASS MEMBERS

Learning objectives or aims are specific changes you desire to
take place in the lives of your learners. Learning objectives serve
several good purposes:

A. If you have objectives, you can measure learning by how many goals you reach during the teaching/learning experience.

B. Unreached objectives can tell you either that your aims are unrealistic or general, or that your methods for reaching them are inadequate.

C. Reached objectives are rewarding and add to one's positive self-image as a teacher. They also serve as encouraging memories when a later struggle in teaching seems too difficult.

When setting learning objectives, the focus is on the behavior change. You ask, "What do I want my adults to *do* differently as a result of this session?" The answer to that question will serve as the basis for your learning objectives.

In order to be effective, behavioral objectives must be *observable, ownable* and *reachable*. An objective must be *observable* so that the teacher can see and/or measure the desired change. An objective must be *ownable* so that the learner will readily agree that the stated change is desirable in his life. An objective must be *reachable* so that it is within the capacity of the learner to achieve successfully.

With a central truth clearly in view, you can now write measurable, ownable and reachable learning objectives for the members of your class. Avoid general, vague objectives such as "help the class get closer to the Lord." Put some teeth into the objectives so that both you and your learners will know when they are reached.

For example, Galatians 4:1-20 discusses the believers relationship to God as sons. The central truth might be written, "focusing on the privileges, freedom and responsibilities of being God's sons." On the basis of that statement, the following learning objectives can be written: "List the privileges of being a son of God; Contrast spiritual sonship with slavery to good works; Identify at least two areas in your life where you want to experience the privileges of being God's son."

Notice the specific, measurable quality of these aims as represented in the verbs "list, contrast and identify."

There are basically three kinds of learning objectives. The *cognitive objectives* refer to our goals for the learner to know, understand, or recognize basic, factual information. Traditionally this was the type of learning objective used in the Sunday School. Measurement of whether or not an adult reached a cognitive goal is fairly easy: One may use written or oral reports, feedback, exams, quizzes or interviews.

One of the most frequently used terms in the area of objectives is the term behavioral objectives. Some educators feel that all objectives must be stated in behavioral terms. By this they mean that objectives must be stated in such a way that the teacher can specify exactly what he wants a learner to be able *to do*, under what circumstances, in what length of time, to what degree of skill and other factors. They believe that all learning must be evidenced by changes in outward behavior. Even if there is a change of attitude or understanding, they say, the only way this could be measured would be to see a change in behavior. According to some educators, unless one can observe what the learner does and can measure his performance, there is no valid way of determining the success of any instruction.

For example, let's assume you are teaching a class of young adults the importance of having family devotions. If your objective is "to lead my adults to learn the basic principles of conducting family devotions," your objective would be primarily concerned with imparting information. A behavioral objective, however, stated in terms of what the learner will do, might read: "To engage in a definite time of Bible study and prayer each day for at least 15 minutes with every family member participating," or, "to use the inductive method of Bible study in my family devotions 20 minutes a day for the next week and be able to pass an exam on the portion of Scripture studied with 80 percent correct answers." Objectives such as these have passed the knowledge stage (which is important) and indicate what the learners will do as a result of what they have learned.

To summarize, then, a behavioral objective describes the performance the teacher or instruction is to produce, stated in terms of what the learners will be able to do. Another type of learning objective is called the *affective objective*. These goals deal more with internal responses than with outward actions—the way a person feels, his attitude or appreciation of a subject—and include both negative and positive feelings or attitudes.

An affective goal might be "to lead my adults to a deeper appreciation of the importance and value of having family devotions," or, "to lead my learners to have a more positive interest in the missionary program of our church." While these goals are primarily concerned with an internal attitude or feeling, if the person's attitude has been changed it is likely to be evidenced in an outward change—the family will start having devotions, or the learner will become involved in missions. If the teacher is successful in changing an attitude or feeling, he will probably notice a change in behavior.

Some educators object to exclusive use of behavioral objectives. They say that a change in behavior can come immediately, during the week, or not for a year or two. Thus, it might be impossible for the original teacher to measure the outcome. When one is dealing with subject matter that concerns feelings, attitudes and appreciation—affective goals—there will be many occasions when a person does change and develop new ideas, but the teacher has little opportunity to measure the change in terms of outward behavior.

In Christian education there is one additional factor in the learning process: the Holy Spirit. It is His teaching that will change attitudes, beliefs and feelings. The teacher cannot do it alone. Much of the teaching in Christian education is in the area of affective goals—changing attitudes, feelings and appreciations. And here you as the teacher must rely on the work of the Holy Spirit in the life of the learner.

Whichever kind of objectives you use, tell your adults what the objectives are whenever possible. This will give them a specific goal toward which to work. Sometimes, however, you will not want to tell your learners a particular goal you have set. If you are depending upon a change in behavior in order to indicate an inward change, it might be too easy for the learner to make the change in order to please or impress you. But for the most part, both you and your adults need to know what you hope to accomplish in each lesson.

4. DEVELOP YOUR TOTAL SESSION TEACHING STRATEGY

Once you have an understanding of the objectives of the adult Sunday School (chapter 1) and the principles and distinctives of adult learning (chapters 3 and 4), and have studied the session Scripture, selected a central truth, and written specific learning objectives, it is time to structure the Sunday School class period. The concept of *Total Session Teaching* implies that the structure for the class session be arranged so that everything that happens, from the time the learners walk into the classroom until the closing prayer, contributes toward the objectives for that session.

The chief obstacle to the *Total Session Teaching* plan is the traditional approach to adult Sunday School—an opening song or two, announcements, special music, more announcements, devotional, offering, and prayer (not necessarily in that order!). The opening session often takes up to half the class time, leaving a frustrated teacher 20-30 minutes for the lesson. The opening session activities usually have little bearing on the lesson topic. This approach results in a fragmented hour.

To accommodate *Total Session Teaching*, offerings may be collected as people enter or leave the classroom, announcements may be mimeographed and distributed at the end of the session, and other activities used only as they contribute to the learning objectives for the session. So move the opening session to the side for a moment and imagine that you have 60 minutes for your class session. The following four-step structure provides an excellent way to utilize the total session for meeting your lesson learning objectives.

A. Fellowship

Every class session should begin with a time of informal fellowship (5-10 minutes) to help people relax, open up and get acquainted. This time of fellowship should be more than just a cup of coffee, a donut and idle conversation about the weather, the kids or last week's big game. In order to get beyond surface conversation, a resourceful teacher will structure some kind of fellowship activity which helps people open up to each other in a nonthreatening way.

Here are three ways to utilize the fellowship period for maximum benefit: 1. Have class members gather in clusters of three or four and share one experience when they were lonely and how they handled it. 2. Have class members gather in pairs. Ask each person to describe to his partner one Christian he knows who is a model Christian in a certain area (humility, generosity, etc.). 3. Have class members share their answers to this question in groups of three or four: "What color best describes this past week for me and why?"

So bring in the coffee and donuts if they are appropriate for your class, but be sure to have a fellowship activity prepared to stimulate meaningful sharing. This kind of fellowship helps to create an atmosphere of warmth and acceptance which is a fitting prelude to purposeful learning.

B. Approach to the Word

This step in the session plan is critical because it is designed to capture the interest of your class and introduce the theme of the session. The Approach to the Word activity (5-10 minutes) seldom involves the learners with the Scripture portion to be studied, but rather whets their appetites so that each person is ready to dig into the Bible for some answers.

For example, if the session Scripture was Matthew 5:21-26 (Jesus' teaching equating a hateful attitude with murder), an Approach activity might involve a brief discussion about the term "justifiable homicide" or a word association exercise on the word "manslaughter." A lesson on faith and fear from Mark 4:35-41 might be introduced by people discussing their phobias. A lesson on the cities of refuge from Joshua 20 could be introduced by having learners fill in an acrostic for the letters of the word "refuge." Such activities turn the heads of the learners in the direction which the Bible study will take them.

C. Exploration of the Word

The Exploration of the Word (20-40 minutes) is the heart of the class session because it involves each learner directly in the study of God's Word. It is during this period that you invite the class members to discover what the Bible passage says and means. The methods you choose for this section of the session plan are successful if you involve the learners in discussing, listing, comparing, researching, prioritizing, analyzing, paraphrasing or otherwise handling God's Word for themselves.

D. Conclusion and Decision

After having spent the majority of the class time in discussing with each other what God's Word says and means, each learner needs to apply the truths of Scripture to his own life. Here each individual deals with the questions, "What does the Bible mean to me and how can I put it into practice in my own life?" The Conclusion and Decision activity (5-10 minutes) may be so personal in nature that you will not ask them to share their discoveries with each other. At some times, however, you will ask learners to gather in small groups and report how the Scriptures studied during the Exploration activity apply to their personal relationships to God and others.

Total Session Teaching is effective when the teacher molds the four session parts into a cohesive unit with each separate part enhancing the others. This plan is successful in the teaching ministry because it cooperates with God's laws for learning and dovetails with the objectives of the adult Sunday School.

We've all seen the poster with the words "Plan Ahead" printed in badly spaced letters. We chuckle because it's obvious that the artist did not plan ahead as his sign admonishes. Planning a Sunday School session is often like the poster—we talk about its importance, but often find ourselves at 11:30 PM on Saturday night grasping for three points and an illustration to use in place of a well-planned lesson.

Hopefully you have seen that careful planning will make a measurable difference in the success of your Sunday School session.

SOME QUESTIONS TO CONSIDER

1. What are the four basic steps in session planning? Which of these steps are you already following?

2. Why is it important for learning objectives to be observable, ownable and reachable?

3. Distinguish between the three basic types of learning objectives.

4. What are the benefits of *Total Session Teaching* over the traditional approach to adult Sunday School?

Using Bible Learning Activities

The basic task of the Sunday School at any age level is to teach learners how to apply Bible truths to their own lives. We have already seen that the teaching/learning process is best served when the learners are actively involved in the process. But any one method of teaching used repeatedly soon loses its effectiveness and leads to boredom in the class. However, if you use variety in your teaching style and involve your learners in discovering and applying Bible truths to their own lives, the Bible will be exciting to study and relevant to the learner's life.

Bible learning activities are the various methods by which the effective teacher involves his class members in Bible study. Let's examine the phrase, Bible learning activity. *Activity* means that the learner is active in the learning process, not passive. It does not mean involving adults in meaningless "fun and games," busy work or activity for activity's sake. The activities chosen must contribute to meeting the learning objectives or they are of no value.

Learning indicates that the purpose of the activity is to cause learning to take place. Remember, in adult Christian education learning is any change which contributes to Christian maturity in an individual. Therefore, a Bible learning activity should contribute toward changing the believer into the image of Jesus Christ.

Finally, it is a learning activity which is centered in the *Bible*. A Bible learning activity is a task which cannot be completed without examining God's point of view.

CHOOSING THE BEST METHOD

When you choose a Bible learning activity, remember that your choice should be based on

- the objective or purpose of the session
- the length of time available
- the equipment and facilities available
- understanding of the ways adults learn
- the needs and interests of your class members
- your own ability to use a particular method.

Bible learning activities are appropriate for all four of the sections of the Total Session Teaching plan. To illustrate, three examples are presented below for each of the four session parts—Fellowship, Approach to the Word, Exploration of the Word, Conclusion and Decision.

Fellowship

Notice how each of the following activities stimulate conversation between class members and encourage the building of positive relationships. This is the purpose of the Fellowship activity.

1. Tape a length of butcher paper to the chalkboard and letter on it, "Today I am..." Have class members use a felt marker to finish the sentence on the sheet any way they wish.

2. Have learners write the name of a Bible character they admire on a stick-on name tag. Have them mingle randomly, explaining what it is they admire about the person they have chosen.

3. Have class members discuss the following question in groups of three or four: "What is my favorite hymn and why?"

Approach to the Word

The following activities are designed to capture the learner's attention and whet his appetite for the Bible study to follow.

1. Ask your learners to brainstorm several talents that people possess. Write their suggestions on the chalkboard.

2. Write the following statement on the chalkboard, flipchart or overhead transparency: "It's harder to live a life of purity today than 20 years ago." Have class members decide whether they agree or disagree with the statement and why.

3. Have class members neighbor-nudge (talk to the person next to them) and share something about anger.

Exploration of the Word

In each of the exercises below the learners are challenged to dig into the Word themselves, exploring the content and discovering the meaning. In each case, the teacher *could* lecture the material. But in telling the lesson content the teacher would rob the learners of the joy of discovery and the lasting learning which results from personal involvement with the Word.

1. Have groups read Galatians 6:7-9 and make a collage depicting the harvest which is desired in the lives of believers.

2. Instruct learners to paraphrase (write in their own words) Romans 12:1,2 so that a 10-year-old child could understand these verses.

3. Assign John 17 to several groups. Have each group list the requests which Jesus made of God in His prayer. Compare the lists.

Conclusion and Decision

Each of the following assignments encourages learners to apply the truths of Scripture to their own lives.

1. Instruct individuals to write letters to God expressing their desire for purity in their lives based on 1 Thessalonians 4:1-8.

2. Write the following statements on the chalkboard: "One thing I need to remember from this session is..." "One thing I need to do as a result of today's Bible study is..." Have each person complete the statement on a sheet of paper and share it in groups of three or four.

3. Provide pencils and paper for everyone. Ask your learners to close their eyes and imagine that Jesus has come into their

lives and is looking at them the way He looked at the Temple at Passover time in John 2. Ask, "If Jesus were to 'clean house,' what habits, attitudes or desires would He overturn and cast out in your life?" Have people share their answers and close in prayer for one another.

EVALUATING YOUR METHODS

Here are several criteria by which you should evaluate the Bible learning activities you are considering for any session. If after evaluation the methods selected do not seem appropriate, adapt them or change them until they meet the learning objectives you have outlined.

1. The method should help direct the learner's attention to the specific nature of the learning task so that he will know what is expected of him. Is he expected to discuss, ask questions, give opinions or write? Let him know what you expect him to do.

2. A method should arouse interest and motivate the individual to learn the subject being presented. Does the method put the class member to sleep or make him sit up and say, "I want to know more about what you just said"? Does it make him eager and ready to respond?

3. A method should also be able to *maintain* interest. When more of the senses (hearing, seeing, etc.) are involved, the person's interest will be greater.

4. A method should let the learner know how he is doing as he attempts to learn the material. This is called "immediate feedback"—the person receives information that tells him how he is progressing. Some methods make this possible, others do not. Discussion, testing and programmed textbooks are some of the methods that do provide feedback.

5. Whenever possible, a method should allow an adult to progress at his own rate. Individual study such as through the use of programmed textbooks encourage such independent study.

6. A good teaching method avoids causing excessive frustration or failure on the part of the learner. Any method that continuously frustrates him or does not allow him to be successful in what he is doing is not effective. Do your learners understand the terms you use? Are your visuals clear and accurate? Are your instructions clear?

7. A teaching method should help the person transfer what he has learned to his everyday life outside of class. You are presenting biblical content so that lives will be changed, not only during that class session but also during the other 167 hours of the week.

"Skillful adult educators have always taken care to see that new concepts or broad generalizations were illustrated by life experiences drawn from the learners. But numerous recent studies on the transfer of learning and the maintenance of behavioral change indicate the desirability of going even farther, and actually building into the design of learning experiences provision for the learners to plan—and even rehearse—how they are going to apply their learnings to their day-to-day lives."[1] Helping a person learn the principles and skills of witnessing will not be accomplished by simply lecturing to him. Demonstration and roleplaying *will* help him transfer learning to his everyday experiences.

8. A method will be more effective if it is not overused. If you use the same method every week, your adults will become bored with it.

9. A method should help develop and maintain positive attitudes toward the teacher, the subject being taught and toward the learner himself.

CATALOG OF BIBLE LEARNING ACTIVITIES

The following is a comprehensive list of Bible learning activities organized into general categories, which you can use to involve your adults in Bible exploration, discovery and application. Any of these activities may be adapted for use with the four parts of the Total Session Teaching plan—Fellowship, Approach to the Word, Exploration of the Word, Conclusion and Decision.

You can use this list when planning your Bible study session much like you use a catalog when shopping for household goods. Scan the list, category by category, to see which Bible learning activity could best be adapted to serve your learning objectives. Remember, the Holy Spirit knows which activities are appropriate; ask His direction as you make your selections.

Discussion

Agree-Disagree ■ A series of purposely controversial statements on a given subject. Class members indicate whether they agree or disagree with the statements and why.

Brainstorming ■ Class members suggest as many ideas as possible on a subject, withholding evaluation until all ideas are presented.

Buzz Groups ■ Small groups (4-8 persons) discuss a given topic for a limited period of time.

Can of Worms ■ Questions or statements on provocative issues are written on separate slips of paper and placed in a container. Groups draw a "worm" from the "can" and respond to it.

Case Study ■ Real-life problem situations are presented; class members analyze the problems and suggest solutions.

Circle Response ■ Each person in turn gives his response to a question or statement presented. No one may comment except during his turn.

Colloquy ■ Small group members present questions about a problem to selected resource persons. The resource persons answer the questions and present additional relevant information.

Debate ■ Speakers holding opposing views on a controversial subject present their views while the audience observes.

Forum ■ Open discussion which follows a formal presentation such as a debate, interview, lecture, panel, sermon, symposium, etc.

Group Response Team ■ Several class members interrupt a

speaker periodically to request immediate clarification of issues.

In-basket ■ Learners are given a situation in which they must respond by setting priorities.

Interview ■ Learners ask specific questions of a resource person.

Listening Teams ■ Several small groups, each given specific questions to answer, listen to a presentation and then express their answers to the large group.

Neighbor-nudge ■ Class members discuss a given question or subject in pairs for a short period of time.

Panel ■ Several qualified persons discuss given topic while an audience observes and listens.

Picture or Statement Response ■ Class members are given a picture (photograph, cartoon, etc.) to look at or a statement to read. Each person gives a sentence response to the picture or statement.

Question and Answer ■ Teacher guides class members into a given topic or Scripture by asking a variety of specific questions.

Screened Speech ■ Several small groups devise questions for an expert in a given field. The expert's speech is given in response to the questions asked.

Talkback ■ Class members respond to a film, demonstration, lecture, etc., by discussing it in their small groups.

Word Association ■ Learners are asked to share the first thoughts which come to mind at the mention of a key word.

Writing

Abridged Edition ■ Individuals or groups read a section of Scripture, then condense it to its basic meaning.

Acrostic ■ Learners use each letter of a key term as the first letter for other words which relate to the key term (i.e., Jesus, Others, Yourself).

Graffiti ■ Class members write brief responses regarding the session topic on a sheet of butcher paper taped to the wall.

Group Writing ■ A small group of learners work together to complete a writing assignment (story, script, report, etc.).

Letter Writing ■ Class members express session truths by writing letters to God, to Bible characters, etc.

List ■ Individuals or groups itemize specific ideas on worksheets or poster paper.

Log/Diary/Journal ■ Learners gain insights into the feelings and attitudes of biblical characters by writing imaginary entries in their daily logs.

Memo ■ Class members apply Scripture truths by writing brief memos to themselves summarizing their responses to the lesson.

News Story/Headline ■ Learners summarize Bible events in headlines or report about them in imaginary news stories.

Open-ended Story ■ Small groups are given unfinished stories and asked to complete them in order to resolve the story situation on the basis of scriptural principles.

Outline ■ Learners list the main points of a Scripture passage in outline form.

Parable ■ Individuals or groups are asked to write a modern-day parable to illustrate a scriptural truth.

Parallel Story ■ Learners write a contemporary story to parallel a scriptural event.

Paraphrase ■ Learners rewrite Scripture verses or hymns in their own words.

Personalized Verses ■ Individuals rewrite key verses using their own names and/or personal pronouns.

Poetry ■ Several varieties of poetry—rhyming and non-rhyming—may be used to respond to a scriptural truth.

Prayer ■ Written prayers help learners verbalize their communication to God more concretely.

Scrambled Verses or Statements ■ Key verses or statements may be scrambled on the chalkboard and teams asked to write them in correct order on worksheets or poster paper.

Silent Film Scripting ■ Small groups make or view a silent film, then write a script which makes the film into a resource for the session objectives.

Telephone Number ■ Learners translate key verses into telephone numbers for easy recall (i.e., Galatians 6:1-5 becomes GA 60105).

Art

Advertisement Brochure ■ Groups design a colorful folder promoting a session concept.

Banners ■ A key thought or verse from the session may be lettered on a banner made of shelf paper or butcher paper.

Bulletin Boards ■ A classroom bulletin board could be divided between small groups who decorate their section to correspond with the session theme.

Bumper Sticker ■ Succinct scriptural reminders can be lettered on strips of paper in bumper sticker fashion.

Cartoon Strip ■ A biblical story or contemporary application of Bible truth may be illustrated by several frames of cartoons using simple stick figures.

Charts ■ Class members graphically display points of information with charts made on poster paper.

Coat of Arms ■ Individuals illustrate specific aspects of their life or the life of a Bible character by drawing three or four sections on a shield as a coat of arms.

Collage ■ An artistic composition made of various materials such as paper, wood or cloth glued on a picture surface.

Doodles ■ Learners respond to a song, story or lecture by doodling designs or pictures which correspond to what they hear.

Frieze ■ A series of drawings or pictures which tell a chronological or continuing story.

Group Drawing ■ Class members participate in making a drawing together which expresses a group opinion or discovery.

Jeremiah Graph ■ Groups read a historical narrative and graph the ups and downs of the Bible characters.

Magazine/Newspaper Tear ■ Learners tear words and/or pictures from periodicals to represent personal feelings or opinions.

Mobile ■ Pictures, shapes or emblems may be used to create a mobile signifying a scriptural insight.

Montage ■ A composite picture made by combining several separate pictures.

Murals ■ Groups work together to create a large painting or drawing on butcher paper depicting a biblical event or practical application of Scripture.

Paintings ■ Water colors or poster paints are effective media for individuals who wish to paint a realistic or impressionistic scriptural truth.

Puppets ■ Learners present Bible characters or scriptural characteristics through the use of puppets.

Rebus ■ A Bible verse or session truth may be presented by drawing a series of pictures which relate the words phonetically.

Slides ■ Groups create original slides (photographic, write-on or ink transfer) to be presented with live or recorded music or narration.

Stained Glass Picture ■ Learners design a meaningful stained glass window effect by gluing scraps of construction paper or colored cellophane to poster paper.

Symbolic Shape ■ Learners cut or tear shapes from paper which symbolize a session truth.

Time Line ■ Class members work together to visualize biblical events chronologically on worksheets or a length of butcher paper on the wall.

Word Poster ■ Learners cut or tear descriptive words or phrases from magazines or newspapers and glue them on poster paper in a meaningful shape.

Drama

Choral Reading ■ Groups write and/or read a prepared script in unison.

Dramatic Reading ■ Learners are assigned different parts of a Scripture narrative or prepared script and read their parts dramatically.

Interview ■ Bible events come alive when an on-the-spot reporter presents an imaginary interview with biblical/historical characters.

Litany ■ Leader and group read or recite aloud a script or prayer responsively.

Living Sculpture ■ Learners interpret scriptural events or concepts by assuming statuelike poses which class members discuss.

Movies ■ Learners make their own 8mm movies out of class to illustrate a session truth.

Pantomime ■ Learners act out a situation without speaking.

Play Reading ■ Class members read a play aloud and then discuss it.

Psychodrama ■ Individuals act out their own life situations in order to gain insight into their feelings and behavior patterns.

Roleplay ■ Learners are given specific problem situations to act out extemporaneously.

Skit ■ Groups plan and act out a situation which relates to the session.

Tableau ■ Learners write and present stylized scenes from a biblical story.

This Is Your Life ■ Class members review the life of a biblical character by presenting imaginary interviews of people who knew him.

TV Show ■ Learners use the format of current television programs to convey session truths.

Music

Commercial Jingle ■ Groups write new words to the tunes of contemporary commercial jingles to present a message from the session Scripture.

Hymn/Song Paraphrase ■ Groups write the message of a hymn or song in their own words.

Hymn/Song Response ■ Learners sing or listen to a hymn or song and tell what it means to them.

Hymn/Scripture Comparison ■ Groups investigate hymns in the light of their scriptural content.

Hymn/Song Rewrite ■ Learners write new words for a familiar tune which express a biblical concept.

Original Hymns/Songs ■ Musically inclined groups write original music and lyrics based on a session truth.

General

Assignment/Project ■ Groups complete specific work or study tasks during a class period or at home.

Census/Survey ■ Learners gather a wide range of personal knowledge and opinion data by asking questions verbally or through written questionnaires.

Demonstration ■ Individuals demonstrate specific tasks or skills; observers practice what they have seen.

Displays/Exhibits ■ Individuals examine certain objects or materials which correlate to a session theme.

Field Trip ■ Learners travel outside the classroom to a location which is of interest.

Games ■ Real-life situations are reproduced in a game format so that learners can simulate their feelings, responses, etc.

Lecture/Monologue/Sermon ■ A prepared verbal presentation given by a qualified individual.

Memory ■ Class members memorize selected Scripture passages or other related material.

Oral Reports ■ Individuals share the results of their research with the class.

Problem Solving ■ Learners are presented a problem to solve which will lead to a better understanding of the session theme.

Programmed Learning ■ A written lesson in which class members answer questions in a step-by-step fashion with sufficient repetition to insure learning.

Puzzles ■ Learners become involved with the session theme by solving puzzles (crossword, word search, scrambled verse or statement, etc.).

Recordings ■ Learners respond to prerecorded songs, lectures or dialogues.

Research ■ Class members participate in in-depth personal or group study using the Bible, commentaries, concordance, dictionary, encyclopedia, etc., both in and outside of class.

Seminar ■ A group convenes for research study under the leadership of an expert.

Symposium ■ A series of speeches given by speakers who present selected and related problems.

Testing ■ Leaders ask for written or oral responses to questions as a means of measuring learning.

Visual Aids ■ Facilities which involve the sense of sight in the teaching/learning process (chalkboard, flipchart, overhead projector, videotape, filmstrips, charts, maps, diagrams, worksheets, demonstrations, etc.).

Workshop ■ A group of learners with a common interest meets together to explore one or more aspects of a topic.

SOME QUESTIONS TO CONSIDER

1. What do we mean by the term *Bible learning activity*?
2. What are some criteria by which a teacher should choose and evaluate Bible learning activities?
3. Select five Bible learning activities from the "catalog" which you could utilize in your class right away.

FOOTNOTE

1. Malcolm Knowles, *The Modern Practice of Adult Education* (New York: Association Press, 1970), p. 45.

Conducting Effective Discussions

Most people like to talk! When we talk with others we are sharing ourselves by sharing our ideas, opinions, doubts, fears and even our dreams. So, when people listen to and accept what we are saying, they are in some ways accepting and affirming us. For this reason, the discussion method is an invaluable tool not only for exploring Bible truths but also for building positive interpersonal relationships.

In a discussion setting adults explore, share and discover meaning or answers. Discussion emphasizes learner initiative, reflective thinking and creative expression. It provides for an interchange of information or opinions guided by a competent leader. It is not a method whereby all of the answers are given by the teacher. When properly related to the objective of the lesson, discussion can be one of the finest methods for teaching adults.

The art of good discussion is tied directly to the art of asking good questions. Why are questions so important? Carefully worded questions provoke thought, trigger remembering and cause people to wrestle with possible answers to problems and situations, thus forming a basis for meaningful discussion. Good questions should move adults beyond mere facts to new understanding as they reason, solve problems and make judgments. Questions should also help adults relate Scripture to contemporary problems. They should be pertinent and complex enough so that they cannot be answered by a simple yes or no. Beginning a question with "What about...?" or "How about...?" encourages students to get involved.

Often a teacher may want to ask an *information question*. This is done to obtain additional facts or more details. "What were some of the miracles that Jesus performed and what were the characteristics of those miracles?"

A *clarifying question* asks the student to repeat what he said in a way that will help both teacher and class members understand what he means. "John, are you saying that..." or "Do you mean that...?"

A *summary or reflective question* may be used when you want to briefly summarize or expand what has just been said. Some class members may take several minutes and countless phrases to make a point. But the teacher can condense this in question form and then ask if his restatement of the question or discussion is correct. "If I understand what we have been saying....Is that what we mean?"

Here are some guidelines to follow when you use questions to stimulate discussion:

1. *Plan your questions.* Your questions should be carefully planned and written down before class time. This assures you of better communication and avoids time-wasting clarifications.

2. *Avoid questions which can be answered yes or no.* "Does the Holy Spirit give gifts to Christians?" "Are Christians supposed to love the world?" These questions require little effort—a good guess has a 50-50 chance! Rather, ask questions that make a learner express himself in his own words. "What are some of the gifts the Holy Spirit gives to Christians?" "What does it do to a Christian when he loves the world?" If a yes-no question is appropriate, be sure to add "Why?" so that some thought is required.

3. *Avoid questions that box the learner in.* If you ask "Why is Moses a person we would want to be like?" a learner, in order to answer, may be forced to violate his own conviction that Moses

is not a person he would want to be like. Instead ask, "What are some qualities in Moses that a Christian might want to emulate?"

4. *Ask the right questions.* If you ask an opinion question you must accept *all* answers, because you asked for opinions. An opinion question is like this one, "How would you describe an ideal wife?" On the other hand, if you ask a fact question you are looking for the *right* answer. A fact question sounds like this, "What characteristics does 1 Peter 3:1-12 say an ideal wife has?" If you want facts, don't ask opinion questions. If you want learners' opinions, don't ask fact questions.

5. *Have a strategy.* Ask questions which move to a goal. There are three stages of questions to use in Bible study. The *first stage* is a question calling for *knowledge*, for the recalling and stating of facts. This question asks, "What does this verse say?" Once learners understand the facts, you can move on to the *second stage*, questions for *comprehension*, or explaining the facts. "What does this verse mean?" When learners have grasped the meaning, you can move on to the *third stage*—*application* internalizing the facts. "What does this verse mean in your life?" The questions in these three stages are building blocks, and each is essential to the next one. A person who does not know the facts cannot understand the meaning. A person who does not understand the meaning cannot explain how to apply it to life.

6. *Give learners time to think.* You may have an answer or an opinion already framed in your mind—but your learners have just heard the question for the first time. Give them a chance to pull together an answer. If they misunderstand the question, rephrase it to help get the answer you want.

7. *Be aware of "spin off" questions.* Your learners' answers to a question may introduce another area you would like to explore with them. Be ready to construct questions on the spot to cover these new thoughts. However, you will want to be sure that the spin-off discussion is not only *interesting* but also is of relevance to the objectives for the session. If it is not, then you may want to

write down the idea and use it in a later discussion where it is more relevant.

8. *Use clarifying questions liberally.* A clarifying question invites the student to "tell us more" about a subject under discussion. "What do you mean? Can you give us some examples? What else can you tell us?" Such questions not only draw out more information but cause the individual asked, and the entire class, to evaluate and to increase its understanding of the subject.

Sometimes a group discussion begins to lag, as if class members aren't sure just where next to take the discussion. At other times the discussion may be quite intense and involved, but the discussion is stuck on a minor point rather than proceeding to the main concept. A teacher can provide assistance by rephrasing or rewording the issue.

Here is an example of how a typical question could be reworded to stimulate discussion. Suppose the question were, "God asked Abraham to do what?" In the first place the question is vague. Second, if the learner knew the answer it simply would be a matter of repeating a previously learned or memorized answer. However, by rewording the question such as, "What shocking command did God give Abraham? What in Abraham's private life made this command particularly difficult to obey? What promise of God seemed to be broken in this command to Abraham?" the adult not only remembers but also is made to think and evaluate. The question could be rephrased again in order to help the learners apply the lesson to everyday situations. Some decisions Christians must make seem clear-cut, between an obvious right and wrong. Abraham, however, had to choose between two seeming wrongs: disobey God or kill his son. Can you think of decisions people must make today between two apparent wrongs? How can one decide which of the two wrongs to do? Do we ever 'do right in doing wrong'? Questions such as these help learners grow in their faith by thinking through problems and scriptural teaching for themselves.

Ask questions which lead to positive or constructive answers. Emphasize the positive things that people can do or say and play down the negative or failure side of life. Ask questions which help people decide what they can do *now*.

Decide in advance how long the class session will last. If this is a Sunday School class, your time is set for you. Keep this limitation in mind so you can spend the last few moments of class summarizing the lesson. You may want to have such a loose structure that you spend the entire time on one question, or you may limit specific topics to 10 or 15 minutes.

LISTEN!

The most important single function performed by a discussion leader/teacher is *listening*. Listening is important for both teacher and student. By listening, a person becomes aware of the thought processes of another person. A person is able to listen attentively and with understanding when he does not feel he has to influence or change the opinion of the person speaking. Listen with the attitude of "Let-me-see-if-I-understand-your-point-of-view-or-what-you-believe," instead of "You-should-believe-what-I-believe-about-that-passage-of-Scripture."[1]

Listening involves risk because by listening a teacher encounters the possibility of being changed. When you teach you may be exposing your ideas and attitudes to those which oppose your own. As you listen to your adults share *their* views, it is possible your own views may be altered. The mark of a quality teacher is the ability to admit that there is much he does not know and is willing to learn from the insights and wisdom of others.

The teacher listens to his class members for these reasons:

▪ When the teacher listens, class members feel their contributions are of sufficient value and worth to be accepted by everyone.

▪ When a teacher listens, the class members will make greater efforts to express their thoughts clearly, knowing that others *are* listening and want to hear what they have to say.

■ If people know that someone may reflect their ideas back to them for clarification, they will make a greater effort to be understood on the first reply.

■ As a teacher listens, class members will be more open-minded to new ideas and understandings. They will be more flexible in their thinking and reasoning.

■ When a teacher listens, adults are more likely to alter their own point of view and admit that the teacher or others may have information that is more in line with the teachings of the Scriptures. Defensiveness will diminish and class members will come with the attitude of seeking other viewpoints as well as authoritative teaching.

■ When a teacher listens, class members will begin to listen to *each other* with more understanding.

■ When a teacher listens, he will learn much that he never knew before.

Take time to understand the questions your class members ask. This rule is frequently violated by both novice and veteran teachers. What do you *think* about when someone asks a question? Do you really listen to the words and try to decide the meaning of the question? Or are you busy thinking what you will say next? By doing this you miss the content of the question. Often you may need to rephrase the question in order for both you and your students to have a proper understanding of what was asked. If you don't understand the question, say, "I'm sorry, I didn't understand. Could you please repeat what you said?"

Do not answer a question too soon. Could the question be answered by the person who asked it or by another class member? Could it be answered by research during the class period or discussion time? Giving a person the answer too soon may dampen his initiative for seeking the answer himself.

Sometimes the problem expressed in a question is not the real problem that's troubling the adult. In this case you might say, "Why do you ask?" or "I wonder if there's a specific instance or situation that causes you to ask that question." In one class studying Romans 13, a class member asked, "Do you think we have to obey the government all of the time?" Instead of stating, "Yes, I think the Scripture very definitely states this," the teacher asked, "You're wondering if there might be exceptions to some of the laws, perhaps in light of our relationship to God and His teachings?" This helped to create an atmosphere where the person's *real* questions could be revealed.

GUIDELINES FOR LEADING A DISCUSSION

1. Be enthusiastic and friendly. Set an open and honest atmosphere. The first words you say will either spark interest or stifle the group. Before you start to talk know what you are going to say and why! Learn the names of the individuals as quickly as possible. If the class is large use name tags. Whenever a contribution is made by a class member, accept it and use it in the way in which it was intended.

2. Be careful how *much you* talk. Tape record a class session and listen to the tape to determine which class members did the talking and how much you commented. Good discussion leaders do not talk more than 30 percent and it is best to limit your comments to about 20 percent.

3. Know who leads the group. Is it the class or you, the leader? Be sure you can lead the group. Questions are one of the better devices for this purpose. We learn as questions are asked. If you feel that a person could contribute more than he has, question him and draw out his ideas. If others sit calmly by looking passive and uninvolved, ask them what they think about the question or comment made by another. "Bob, what do you think of Ann's statement? Do you agree? Why?"

4. Know what size group will be best for the discussion session and limit the group to that size. Groups of 8 to 20 are usually most effective for discussion. The more controversial the issue, the smaller the group should be, because most of the people will

have personal viewpoints and ideas to express and debate.

5. Relate the discussion to the Scriptures. Don't let the discussion become simply a time for pooling everyone's ignorance! See what the Bible says.

6. Encourage each person to contribute his ideas. Ask for contributions by name. For example, "We haven't heard from Jim yet, and I think he has been doing some real thinking about what has been said here this morning. Jim, what about it? What do you think? We'd like to know." Give a person good reason to participate.

7. Do not argue, especially if you are asking for people's opinions. *Lead* them to the correct answer or rely upon other class members to assist you. A discussion teacher who is judgmental or critical is a detriment. Let them see that you want to know how they *really* feel. Watch your tone of voice.

8. Welcome a pause or silence. Most teachers become very uncomfortable with silence, but it usually means the adults are thinking. There is value in silence. Some teachers let a class sit for three or four minutes waiting until one of the class members ventures an opinion.

9. Do not let one or two members control the group by doing all the talking. *You* are the leader. Thank the talkative members for their contributions and suggest that now you would like to hear what the others have to say. Or limit the number of contributions made by any person until every member has expressed himself. You may want to begin the class with a question and then proceed around the group asking each person to give his personal opinion about the question.

10. Some groups are slower to respond than others. If they seem reticent to contribute their ideas, find out why. It may be the topic (is it a topic that interests them?), the setting (is the group relaxed, tense, physically uncomfortable?), or the leader (do you encourage them to share their ideas?).

11. Keep the discussion on the topic. Everyone enjoys a story or an illustration, but if the story has no bearing on the topic

under discussion it should not be included. If someone gets sidetracked in his discussion let the class know that this is interesting, but "you seem to have strayed a bit from the original question." A timely question, however, may steer the group back to the topic without your having to be so direct.

12. What should you say when someone gives a wrong or irrelevant answer? Should you tell him, "That's wrong," or should you just ignore the statement? No. Simply say, "That's interesting," "Thank you for that," "I've never heard it expressed that way before," "Frankly, what do you think about it?" "Can anyone locate any Scriptures that may assist us here?" or "What do the rest of you think?" and proceed with the discussion.

13. What should you say to the person whose typical response to a question is (a) instantly to quote a Scripture verse as a proof text, (b) to suggest or imply that anyone who does not think as he does is not spiritual, or (c) to state that this problem or situation will be answered by prayer and the best thing to do is to pray about it?

Let your students know that any Scriptures shared must be related to the topic under discussion. Evaluate the verses to see if they apply or if they have been taken out of context. You might say, "Before we look at the Scriptures have we defined or discussed the problem sufficiently?" or "What other Scriptures could be applied that would give the same meaning or even another viewpoint?"

The member who implies or suggests that others are having problems or are not spiritual because they do not think the way he thinks should be confronted gently. Suggest that "We are not here to make judgments about others' beliefs or how they express themselves. We appreciate people being open enough to honestly share their questions, doubts and opinions. As we do this we can all search together to find answers. Perhaps some of the members have progressed further in their thinking and yet some of our own long-held beliefs could be reevaluated to see if they are really what we believe or if they are accurate." "Let's think together before we draw any conclusions. I think we have some honest and interesting thoughts expressed here and they are worthy of deeper study."

The person who immediately suggests prayer as a solution may be very sincere. But there may be other reasons behind his suggestion. Suggest that "Prayer is very important and we should pray. However, I'm not sure that now is the time for prayer. I'm not sure that we have really defined or discussed the problem enough so that we are clear as to what some answers or alternatives might be." "Thank you for the suggestion. What about some of the rest of you? Perhaps you have some other suggestions that we should consider." "I've prayed about similar issues, but I've also found that it is very helpful to discuss the matter fully so that my praying is more perceptive and intelligent."

14. Summarize the discussion at the end of the period and give assignments. Sometimes definite answers and conclusions will have been reached, sometimes not. On some occasions class members will continue to think and study during the week in order to make a final decision.

SUMMARY GUIDELINES FOR DISCUSSION LEADERS

Be Prepared

Make an outline or guide for the discussion (introductions, reactions, specific questions).

List significant questions to stimulate thinking and discussion (unless prepared by a speaker).

Select the proper room for your group and arrange the chairs in a semicircle if possible.

A Good Leader Does:

■ Give everyone an opportunity to express himself.
■ Keep the discussion on the subject.
■ Limit long speeches to short statements.

■ Draw out the members who are reluctant to speak up.

■ Make sure everyone understands the points being made.

■ Turn questions asked of him back to the group.

■ Restate the question when discussion wavers.

■ Summarize the conclusions (if any) of the group and of each group topic.

■ Permit periods of silence for thinking to take place.

■ Always use tact and stay alert.

■ Work for an atmosphere of freedom and honesty in which all viewpoints and comments can be aired without fear or reprisal.

A Good Leader Does Not:

■ Monopolize the discussion.

■ Allow any one member to dominate the discussion.

■ Act as if he has all the answers.

■ Get nervous when there is silence.

■ Answer a question before the group does.

■ Continue the discussion on irrelevant subjects.

■ Permit quarreling.

■ Let wrong conclusions go unquestioned.

■ Pretend to agree when he does not.

■ Hide his own convictions.

■ Oblige the group always to agree with him.

Remember:

■ Have each member introduce himself to the group.

■ Present the purpose and subject of the discussion.

■ Get the discussion started with questions that demand answers—other than yes or no.

■ Tactfully interrupt when people stray from the subject or if someone becomes argumentative; get the discussion back on course.

■ Stick to the subject. Try to insist on first person sharing rather than third person hearsay, sermonizing or speculation.

■ Guide the discussion along profitable lines.

■ Gear the discussion to the personal needs of the individuals.

■ Conclude the discussion, at the designated time, with a constructive summary.

■ Make a brief report to the combined groups (if requested).

VARIATIONS OF DISCUSSION TECHNIQUES

One of the distinct advantages of the discussion method is that it can be used with two people or with two hundred. In addition to small group discussions, there are many variations involving different numbers of people. Each method involves the student in sharing his ideas with others and learning from the other group members. Choose those methods most suitable for your class and the lesson being taught. Avoid using any one method so often that it becomes a boring routine.

Neighbor-nudging

Neighbor-nudging is an informal, effective method of beginning a discussion, or getting quick participation. It simply is a very brief discussion between two people sitting together.

They are given the discussion question with the instructions that they have one minute in which to discuss the question. At the end of that time they must have some answer.

An example might be: "Today, we need to answer a very important question. What do we mean by the term 'teaching'? What is teaching and how would you define it? Please turn to the person next to you or in front or back. Now together, in two's, discuss your answers. We will have just one minute in which to do this. I will call time when the 60 seconds are up. You may begin right...now."

When the minute is up, call time, thank them for participating, and ask people to share their definitions. (Always try to include a report sharing time when people have been asked to do something.)

This simple technique is invaluable for the purpose of getting everyone involved at once or creating immediate interest. A distinct advantage is that there is no limit to the size of the group with which this can be used.

Circle Response

Another method that can be used at the onset or during a group meeting is the circle response. The discussion leader presents a question or statement. Each person, usually in turn, will give his answer or opinion to the question. No one is allowed to respond a second time until each person has contributed. This is used to obtain an opinion from everyone and to consider opinions of others. (If you fear the danger of "hitch-hiking," i.e., simply repeating the opinion of a previous learner, you may ask each person at the beginning to write down his response, then read it when his turn comes.)

It should not be a question that can be answered yes or no, but one that requires a statement by the learner. For example, you might ask:

If you could change one thing about your life right now, what would it be?

What is the most important task facing our church today?

What is the most important portion of Scripture to you?

If you had the power to change one major event in the history of mankind, what would it be? The leader asks either the person on his left or right to begin and then the responding continues around the group. He may then ask if there are any additional comments before he summarizes. This technique may take the entire time or may be used as a prelude to another technique. Generally, it should be limited to smaller groups because of the time involved. Learners do not have to sit in a circle but it helps.

Agree/Disagree Statements

An exciting method of stimulating discussion is the use of the agree/disagree statement. This is simply a statement to which there may be several responses. For example, "In an adult class what the teacher does is more important than what the learner does. Do you agree or disagree with this statement?"

Those who think in terms of the teacher's preparation and presentation will agree. Those who realize that the learner learns more when he discovers it for himself, will disagree—and discussion ensues.

There are several ways to get responses. You may have all those who agree, stand, or raise their hands, or even move to one side of the room. You may discuss each question as you come to it, or you may get the opinions on them all and then go back to those where the greatest spread of opinion seemed to be.

It is also effective to ask those who took a certain position questions such as, "Could you share with us why you believe this statement?" or "Why and upon what do you base your belief?" Still another way is to ask those on the other side to respond to the first person's ideas—let the two groups try to convince each other. As participants change their views, let them move from side to side.

It is very important to phrase the agree/disagree statements carefully so there is room for disagreement. Obvious answers do not provoke discussion. An ideal statement would be one which would divide your groups right down the middle!

Following are some typical agree/disagree statements.

What Do YOU Think?

Agree	Dis-agree	Statement
☐	☐	It is all right to modify the truth to avoid unpleasantness in relationships with others, i.e.: especially when saying something that is true could hurt an individual.
☐	☐	It is a sign of spiritual and emotional immaturity for a Christian to be angry.
☐	☐	The chief value in prayer is the fact that we are able to admit our sins and express our needs verbally, getting them out in the open.
☐	☐	The Bible teaches that God does not change and therefore prayer would not have too much effect upon Him.

The agree/disagree sheet is a very effective way to stimulate discussion. In some groups where the sheet has been used, learners became so involved in the discussion they did not want to end the session. In their search through the Scriptures they found verses they had never read before or verses that had previously had little meaning for them. Some realized through their study and discussion that what they believed about the subject was substantiated by Scripture; others confessed that what they believed was contrary to Scripture.

The wording of the statements forces people to think, to clarify what they *do* believe and commit themselves to that belief (by checking the agree or disagree column, sharing their views and the reasons for their views). The discussion reveals differences of opinion in the group. As the members listen to the reasons for the beliefs of others and the Scriptures presented, they can judge the validity of their own beliefs. The discussion period makes them feel that their opinions are important—someone is interested in what they think. Adults are more likely to express their true views because they do not know beforehand what the consensus of the group will be and thus cannot be swayed by the opinions of others.

The agree/disagree sheet can be used with buzz groups, panels, to begin a lecture series or for general discussion.

Completion Statements

A fourth technique for promoting discussion is the use of sentence completion statements or questions. For example, a phrase "Happiness is..." might be placed on the blackboard or a piece of newsprint and the learners asked to complete it in various ways.

Another plan is to place a series of such incomplete statements on a sheet of paper on which each learner puts his response. An example might be: "An adult learns best when..." After all have completed the statements, sharing the answers stimulates discussion.

This may also be used for a Conclusion activity. For example, the statement might read: "As the result of what I have learned today, I will..." or "Now that I understand what the Bible says, I will have to..."

Roleplaying

In roleplaying the teacher describes a particular situation. The adults choose different roles and act out the situation described by the teacher (without advance preparation). The results of the roleplaying are analyzed and discussed by the rest of the class. This method can be used to help solve problems and make people more aware of the feelings of others.

Here are two roleplaying situations on the subject of witnessing to illustrate how you can use this method with your class.

1. Ask several class members to roleplay a situation in which two Christians call on a typical non-Christian family. They attempt to share their faith with them, only to find that the terminology they are using is unfamiliar to the family.

Example: "Are you saved?" "Have you invited the Son of God into your heart?"

Whenever unfamiliar terms are used, the family asks, "What do you mean by that?" or "I don't know what you mean."

Limit the roleplay to perhaps two minutes so that it does not drag on too long. Then discuss what went wrong in this attempt to witness. This will help your class members realize that in witnessing they must use language that is common to *both* Christian and non-Christian.

Distribute a list of the 10 terms listed below. Ask your class members to define the terms individually or in buzz groups so that a non-Christian would be able to understand them.

Saved	Atonement
Forgiveness	Born again
Grace	Justification
Sin	Prayer
Holy	Love

2. Many adults hesitate to share their faith in Christ with others because they do not know how to do it, or because they have never had a successful witnessing experience. The following roleplay situation will give them firsthand experience.

Ask a class member to volunteer to roleplay the part of an atheist. Seat him in front of the class. Ask for another volunteer to attempt to lead this person to Christ. Usually several people will be willing to try. Let them roleplay the situation for five to eight minutes. During this time no one else can interrupt or make comments.

After the roleplay ask the group to react to what they just saw. Usually someone will say, "Well, I think I would have done it this way." When this happens ask the person to demonstrate rather than tell what he would have done.

After several people have roleplayed the situation, divide the class into groups of three. Within these groups ask one person to take the role of a Christian attempting to witness and one person to take the role of the non-Christian to whom the Christian is witnessing. The third person acts as an observer who will evaluate the roleplay situation.

Allow five minutes for the roleplay, then let the observer tell what he saw and heard. The role of the observer is an important one. He can often see and hear things that will help improve the effectiveness of the person who is witnessing. Then have the person playing the part of the non-Christian tell how he felt about the way the Christian witnessed to him. Continue the roleplays until every person in each group has had an opportunity to play a role at least twice.

Depth Bible Encounter

Each person rewrites the passage of Scripture being discussed in his own words. He may not use any of the words in the Bible text. He then shares his paraphrase with the entire group or within a small group.

Next, ask each person to write his answers to the statement, "If

I took this passage seriously and applied it to my life right now, this is what I would have to do." When the learners have finished writing, ask them to share what they have written with the members of their group. Urge them to commit themselves to following through on applying the Scripture to their lives during the coming week.

SOME QUESTIONS TO CONSIDER

1. What is a discussion?
2. Give an example of a reflective and a clarifying question.
3. What guidelines should you follow in leading a discussion?
4. List three problems that may arise in a discussion and indicate how you would handle each one.
5. Define neighbor-nudging and discuss when this can be used.
6. Write five statements of your own that could be used on an agree/disagree sheet.

FOOTNOTE

1. Two helpful books on this subject are *The Awesome Power of the Listening Ear* by John Drakeford (Word Books), and *Are You Listening?* by Ralph Nichols and Leonard Stevens (McGraw-Hill).

Lecturing Creatively

The lecture is undoubtedly the most frequently used teaching method. You hear at least one lecture every day. When you're sick your physician explains what you must do to get well. A salesman attempts to sell you his product. The television commentator relates the day's news. A teacher explains mathematics. Your pastor preaches a sermon. All of us are familiar with the lecture. In many situations it is a very effective means of communication.

One of the misconceptions about the lecture, however, is the idea that "lecturing equals teaching." Many people believe that "teaching is talking" and "learning is listening." But the two cannot be equated. An adult, bored by an over-used lecture method, tunes out the lecture as his mind wanders miles away. He may *look* attentive, but he isn't learning anything. Because of misuse and overuse of an otherwise effective teaching method, some adults just plain rebel against the idea of sitting through "another lecture class."[1]

When the adult teacher is lecturing, the class atmosphere is teacher-centered, teacher-directed and teacher-dominated. The teacher is at the center of the stage and is actually doing the most learning. Why? Because he is the one most involved in the learning process. People learn most effectively when they are involved and can discuss ideas. But this is not happening during the lecture. Lecture is necessary at times, but it is not the most ideal way to teach adults.

"The lecture, in and of itself, is inadequate for teaching certain types of concepts. Attitudes, skills and feelings are not learned through pure telling or showing procedures. The lecture assumes that students are all equally ready or interested, are all hearing the same thing, will all remember the lecture and can all apply it in the solution of problems. Even at the lecture's best, there seems little relationship between this passive listening role and the problem attack required for effective learning."[2]

In certain situations, however, the lecture is an effective teaching method and has great potential value. The lecture can be used effectively to—

■ Increase the listeners' knowledge and present information in an organized fashion.

■ Help identify and clarify problems and analyze viewpoints.

■ Stimulate, inspire, challenge and motivate.

■ Give the teacher control over the classroom situation.

■ Cover a wide range of material quickly.

■ Give the teacher opportunity to share unusual insights or information that others do not have.

The lecture may also be used when the group is too large to use any other technique effectively.

To be effective, the lecture must be used selectively and for a definite purpose. Listed below are some guidelines to help you know when and how to use the lecture method with your adults. (Some of the ideas presented below have been adapted from the book, *Using the Lecture in Teaching and Training*, by LeRoy Ford [Broadman Press]. Every teacher should study this book.)

PREPARING TO LECTURE

1. Take a look at the content of the lesson you plan to teach. Is the material to be presented factual or demonstrable? Is there a lot of material to cover, such as in a survey course? Do the learners need a broad overview of ideas or events? Is the information technical? If any of these questions can be answered yes, the lecture may be the method you should use. Remember, however, that you can combine methods. Maps, charts and other visuals will greatly reinforce your lecture.

2. Gather sufficient material to make the lecture interesting.

Then organize your main ideas. Will you need to present them in chronological order or some other way? Build upon what your learners know—progress from the known to the unknown. Now prepare an outline listing the main points and the subpoints. Add illustrations to help clarify the points and make transitions between points of the outline.

3. Practice your lecture at home before you present it to the class. Stand in front of a mirror as you talk to see how you appear. Do you slump, lean over the podium, pace back and forth or move around nervously? Tape the lesson and listen to yourself. Or tape a class session and listen to it at home. How do you sound? Do you speak clearly and distinctly? Or do you slur your words, punctuate your talk frequently with *uhs* and *ahs* or with a favorite expression such as "you know," "know what I mean?" or some annoying expression?

How we appear and sound to others is sometimes difficult to observe. Yet if a teacher is serious about becoming a better teacher, he will want to undergo self-examination. Some adult teachers have had their class session videotaped and then listened to and watched themselves in action. These teachers confessed that this was a difficult and painful experience, but most beneficial and they wanted to do it again. They suggested that every teacher should have the opportunity of analyzing his own teaching at least once using the videotape.

4. Use language your students will understand. If your class is full of Ph.D.'s you can get away with a few six-syllable words. But for the most part, stick to simple words that everyone can understand. Vary the pitch of your voice and the rate of speed at which you speak to emphasize a change in ideas. Don't attempt to cover too many points.

PRESENTING THE LECTURE

People learn more and retain more when they have opportunity to respond to a lecture. During a lecture your learners can—

- Take notes.
- Complete a worksheet giving a brief outline of the lecture.
- Serve as listening teams and prepare answers to questions given them before the lecture begins.
- Take an introductory test before the lecture begins to start them thinking about the subject.
- Summarize the lecture with the person sitting next to them during the last five minutes of the class.

Vary your method of presenting the lecture. For example, you can—

- State the main concept or thought of the lesson.
- Ask learners to read the concept from a chart.
- Ask learners to reword the concept.
- Present the necessary information, then give a brief demonstration.
- Tape the material prior to the class and play it during class time.
- List the main ideas of the lecture on index cards and distribute these to students as they arrive; when you reach a particular point in the lecture ask the person who has that card to read it aloud.

A lecture should *always* be accompanied by some kind of visual aid. In most lectures the sense of hearing is the only one of our senses used. Yet we learn through our other four senses as well. Several studies have indicated that the greatest degree of learning and retention takes place when visuals accompany a lecture. The Socony-Vacuum studies revealed that when a class is conducted by using just lecture, students will remember 70 percent of what they heard three hours later. Three days later they will remember only 10 percent. But when students hear a lecture and see visuals which accompany it, they will remember 85 percent three hours later and 65 percent three days later.

Through the Socony-Vacuum research they discovered that people learn 1 percent through taste, 1½ percent through touch, 3½ percent through smell, 11 percent through hearing and 83 percent through sight. They also discovered that adults remember 10 percent of what they read, 20 percent of what they hear, 30 percent of what they see, 50 percent of what they see and hear, 70 percent of what they say as they talk and 90 percent of what they say as they do something.

Another study reported by the 3M Company indicated similar results. Students in a college zoology course were tested 15 months after they had completed the course and they remembered only 28 percent of the technical terms they had learned. But they did remember 78 percent of the facts which were associated with an illustration or picture during the course.

Visual aids are effective with every age group but especially with adults. Adults have a wide range of experience to draw upon and can respond to a visual stimulus and integrate it into their thinking even better than younger people.

There are many visuals you can use with your lecture—charts, maps, diagrams, pictures, the overhead projector. Distribute charts and outlines for your learners to follow. Records, films and filmstrips add interest. A wide variety of visuals are available today. Their use is limited only by a lack of imagination.

Want to be a really good lecturer? Then you must work continually at both the content and presentation of your lectures. As a teacher you are to be an authority and an interpreter of the material. Your presentation should be well done, but the focal point of the class must be the Word of God—not you.

Don't use the lecture for every class session and when you do use it combine it with other methods. "The lecture method is most effective," says Findley Edge, "when it is used along with some other methods . . . . It should be a relatively rare thing for the teacher to use the lecture method for the entire class session."[3]

FIVE VARIATIONS OF THE LECTURE

The lecture can be adapted to provide both variety and involvement on the part of your students.

The *lecture forum* is a lecture followed immediately by total group participation in an open discussion. Questions and reactions are solicited from the class following the presentation and the teacher and class members react together. At the conclusion of the discussion the teacher summarizes the conclusions of the discussion and can give guidelines and suggestions for out-of-class involvement and study.

Use of *listening teams* assures a high rate of listening and involvement. Divide the class into several groups. Give each group specific questions to answer or points to look for in the lecture. After the lecture, ask each group to share its findings. The individual members may also ask the teacher questions about his presentation. Following the discussion the teacher summarizes the contributions of the group and reinforces the main points. He can also suggest a course of action for additional study within or outside of the class.

The *panel* allows several class members or several teachers to share their knowledge about a subject informally before the class. For example, you might ask several members to read a chapter in a particular book during the week, then form a panel to discuss their findings with the entire class. Select panel members on the basis of previously demonstrated interest and competency for some subjects and on the basis of interest for others. The person in charge of the panel (the moderator) prepares a list of questions for the panel members to consider. He may meet with the panel before the class session to clarify the procedure and the discussion itself. The moderator starts the discussion with his questions and helps keep the panel members' give-and-take true to the topic. The other members of the class watch and listen but do not participate verbally.

A *symposium* is a series of short formal speeches representing varying viewpoints on a topic. Members of the symposium do not discuss their views with the other members as in a panel but simply make their own presentations. They too are selected because of their competency in a specific field. The speeches vary in length from 3 to 20 minutes depending upon the number of participants, the topic and the amount of time available. Usually the presentation is one-way with no discussion between speakers or between speakers and class members. However, many teachers feel it is best to vary the approach by allowing open discussion following the presentation.

Still another variation of the lecture method is the *reaction panel*. Several resource persons or class members hold a panel discussion in front of the group following a lecture. They react to the lecture by sharing their insights, reactions and questions.

No doubt you will use the lecture frequently with your adult class. There are times when it is the best method to use. Use it properly and to its best advantage. Remember that the lecture is most effective when it is combined with other methods.

SOME QUESTIONS TO CONSIDER

1. What types of concepts cannot be taught by lecturing?
2. The lecture can be used effectively to...
3. List the steps involved in preparing a lecture.
4. What are the principles to follow in presenting a lecture?
5. Define the following:
   (a) Lecture forum
   (b) Symposium
   (c) Reaction Panel

FOOTNOTES

1. Lois E. LeBar, *Education That Is Christian* (Westwood, N.J.: Revell, 1958), pp. 204,245.
2. Anne Richardson Gayles, "Lecture Vs. Discussion," *Improving College and University Teaching* (Spring, 1966), p. 95.
3. Findley Edge, *Helping the Teacher* (Nashville: Broadman Press, 1959), p. 105.

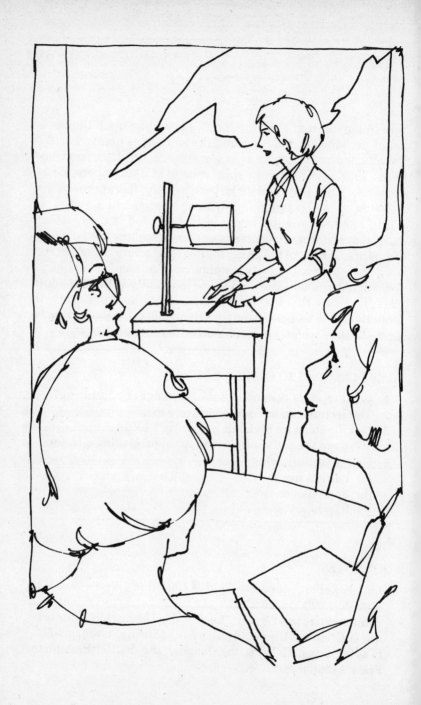

Making the Classroom Functional

"How was your Sunday School class today, Dad?"

Eleven-year-old Ken surprised his father by asking the stock question which the Conrad parents usually posed to Ken and Kris on the way home.

"It was okay," Ed replied. But as his mind quickly replayed the Sunday School hour, only negative things stood out: the room was hot and stuffy, the chairs were junior-sized, only one of the overhead lights worked and the paint was chipping off the bare walls. Furthermore, Ed thought, Sam Barker, the adult teacher, had given the lesson without using the chalkboard or any other visual aids. It took only a few seconds for Ed to realize that his day in Sunday School had been pretty "blah." He could barely remember the lesson topic.

"Ours was neat, Dad," Ken broke into his father's thoughts. "Mr. Lockhart had the room all decorated with some new posters. He had some neat pictures on the flipchart during the lesson. And we got to open the windows and enjoy the cool breeze while we worked on our chariot models."

Ed's adult class had the "blahs" and Ken's sixth grade class had the "neats." A great part of the difference was in the classrooms themselves. Sometimes we forget that adults need attractive and functional classroom facilities just as much as the younger learners. There are at least two good reasons to take great care in providing adequate facilities for adults.

STRATEGIC POSITION OF ADULT DEPARTMENT

The educational facilities for adults are important because the adult department of the Sunday School is strategic to the entire program of the local church. Ironically, provision for adults is often the forgotten element in the church building program. The result: Adults wind up using such places as the pastor's study, the choir loft, the kitchen in the fellowship hall, the sanctuary, the furnace room—almost any place they can be crowded into. This is most unfortunate, for the adult department of the Sunday School can be the key to the numerical growth of the entire school as well as the primary source from which to draw leadership for teaching, superintending, and for filling positions on the various boards and committees in the rest of the church organization.

INVOLVEMENT IN SUNDAY SCHOOL OBJECTIVES

A second reason that the physical facilities are so important is that three of the four objectives of the adult Sunday School take place primarily in the classroom setting. The production of an atmosphere of warmth and acceptance, the provision of sound biblical instruction, and the provision of a framework for transforming biblical truth into living action all take place within the physical setting of the classroom. Our learners don't live in a classroom! They live in a real world made up of relationships, conflicts, temptations, opportunities, constraints, and choices. So, the Bible teacher must begin in a sterile classroom with four bare walls and create an exciting place to learn about God and His Word. That's a challenge! But it is worth the effort in order to create a learning environment which supports and enriches your teaching.

SOME GUIDELINES FOR ADULT FACILITIES

There are certain things to be aware of in planning and creating an adult classroom. Let's take a look at some of those guidelines.

Floor Space

The first thing to be considered is the matter of floor space. Ideally, there should be 10 square feet per person in the classroom. With a class size of 30 members about 300 square feet will be needed in each classroom. The need for maximum involvement in the learning process dictates within broad limits how this 300 square feet should be proportioned. An absurd illustration of this would be a classroom with the dimensions of 5 feet by 60 feet. There would be 300 square feet, all right, but obviously group discussion, circle response, buzz groups, and other such types of group learning experiences would become a comedy of errors and the epitome of chaos and confusion.

On the other hand, a room about 15 by 20 feet would be more flexible and usable for learning purposes. Using one of the 20-foot sides as the "front" of the room would work best.

Location of Rooms

In addition to the amount of floor space planned per person, another consideration should be the location of the classrooms. Some of the age-level needs of adults should be reflected in the choice of location for their classrooms. Rooms for adults with small children are best located near these children's classrooms. Classrooms for older adults are best placed on the ground floor. (An alternative to this would be the installation of an elevator for their use.) Stairs can be a problem for some older members who have health limitations.

Lighting and Ventilation

It is important that classrooms have the proper lighting, heating, cooling and ventilation. It has been suggested that there be an illumination level of 30 foot candles in the classroom, that a temperature of 68-70 degrees Fahrenheit be maintained, and that the rate of ventilation be in the neighborhood of 10 cubic feet of air per adult per minute, while providing 6 to 10 complete changes of air per hour.

Acoustics

Acoustical considerations are also important. The walls of the classroom should be soundproof, the ceiling acoustically treated, and the floor carpeted. Thirty-five to forty decibels have been suggested as the highest acceptable room noise level. Sharp handclaps sounded while the class is in the room should produce no echo. An echo under these conditions means too much reverberation, and additional acoustical treatment would then be necessary. This is particularly important because of the need for moving chairs around for small learning experiences, such as buzz groups, neighbor-nudging, etc.

Storage

Storage space in our classrooms is necessary in the form of a cabinet or some sort of a closet. Chalk, eraser, paper, pencils, and other materials which might be needed during the class session may be kept there.

Up to this point only the permanent or nonmovable aspects of the physical facilities have been discussed. But what about the equipment that goes into this well-planned classroom space?

Chairs and Tables

Certainly there should be sufficient chairs for the number who will be attending the class. They should be movable so that circles, squares, and discussion groups may be formed easily and quickly. Some find it advantageous to buy "tablet chairs" which have a large arm rest suitable for taking notes, stacking books, and so forth.

It will be helpful to the teacher if there is a small table available on which to place his Bible and other teaching materials (not to be used as a podium, however). A second small table or desk can be of help to the secretary as a place to centralize his clerical activities.

Chalkboard/Newsprint Flipchart

Many teachers are handicapped without a chalkboard or newsprint flipchart. Either a permanent or portable one should be provided in the classroom. A tack board or bulletin board also can be a useful teaching tool for displaying visual aids, emphasizing announcements, or describing service projects. If an overhead projector is frequently used, it is well to have a permanent screen in the classroom.

Audiovisuals

Audiovisuals illustrate and reinforce ideas, facts, concepts, events, stories, themes and principles. They aid memorization. They provoke learners to apply scriptural principles in contemporary living. In other words, the more a learner can see and touch in regard to what he is learning, the more we can expect him to remember. Conversely, the more abstract the learning experience, the less we can expect the learner to remember.

Visuals include maps, charts, bulletins, pamphlets, flipcharts, posters, banners, photographs, displays, chalkboard writing, flannelboards, models, slides and transparencies.

Audio aids include records, cassette tapes, etc.

Audiovisual combinations include filmstrips, videotapes, movies, and slide-tape shows.

The use of audiovisual aids such as tape recorders, slide, filmstrip or motion picture projectors, and overhead and/or opaque projectors will necessitate having electrical outlets conveniently placed in the room. There also needs to be an efficient and effective means of darkening the room when using projected visuals and for balancing artificial and natural light. (Overhead projectors, however, can be used effectively without altering the normal room light.)

Seating Arrangement

As you move through the four parts of the Sunday School session, provide carefully chosen activities to involve the adults in learning God's principles. You will find that some learning activities are best accomplished in a large group and others in small groups. So, the class will work all together, or work in small groups as directed by the instructor.

Keep the entire class together for instructions, for their sharing insights and conclusions, for reporting on results of small group assignments, for lecture, panel discussions, debates and other presentations.

Break the class into small work groups for problem-solving discussions to allow each adult opportunity to express his opinion, to work together on a project, and to complete assignments.

The large and small groups can be used in various combinations within the same session. In fact, there are six basic arrangements you might choose from, depending on what you want to accomplish through the lesson. These are shown in the following diagrams.

The learning methods chosen for the session will dictate the classroom arrangement. Is a large group presentation planned? Arrange the chairs in a semicircle (rather than neat, tight, schoolhouse rows!). Are both large and small group assignments planned? Then arrange the chairs in small groups around the room. Are Bible learning methods planned which will require your adults to work at tables? Then provide enough tables with appropriate supplies to accommodate those groups that will need them. If the groups will not need the tables for the entire session and if there is room, you may wish to place the tables around the sides of a room rather than putting a table in the middle of a small group.

It is important to recognize that the arrangement of the equipment within the facilities will have an important effect on creating an atmosphere of warmth and acceptance. The back of heads

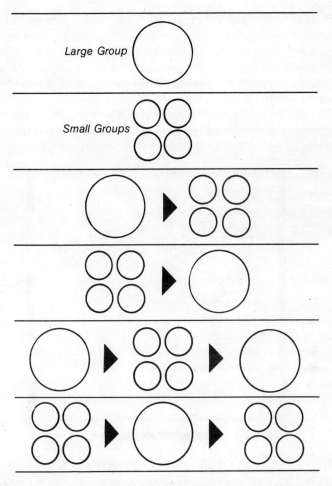

and an occasional profile view do little to promote fellowship and personal interaction among class members. But putting the chairs in a circle helps to create an atmosphere of warmth and acceptance because it allows each person to face another as well as to have his neighbor partially face him. The desired atmosphere of warmth and acceptance can be enhanced even more by breaking the large group up into smaller units for discussion and exchange of ideas. This promotes participation, self-knowledge, and knowledge of the other people in the group as well. Also, it is easier for latecomers to enter these groups if they are already formed before their arrival.

These small groups can meet in different parts of the classroom in what is called an open room arrangement. See the figure below.

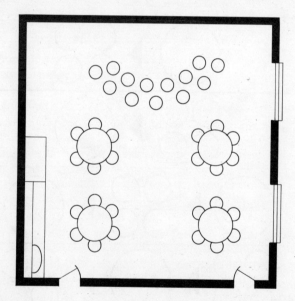

If your educational building is constructed on the assembly/ class design and you would like to implement open room teaching in your class you can adapt your facility. Remove the doors from the small classrooms or allow them to stand open during the teaching session. In addition to assigning small groups to the small classrooms, place two or more activities in the adjoining assembly area at the same time.

PROBLEM FACILITIES

Grouping, learning activities and creative methods may look good in the minds of Sunday School experts who are planning for the ideal situations, but how does the teacher whose class meets in the sanctuary, with fixed pews, handle the whole idea of groups moving around and working on projects that require mobility and creativity?

As we talk about the more ideal situations, we risk falling short of the goal. Nevertheless, when people make plans with the ideal situations in mind, they come much closer toward achieving their goals than if they limit their plans to their immediate situations.

USE YOUR IMAGINATION

Consider the possibilities that exist for imaginative use of the church sanctuary as a center of creative learning among adults:

- ▪ How about using the aisles, the podium area and other free space for chairs and discussion groups?
- ▪ Or have people get into small discussion groups scattered around the auditorium, far enough away from each other that they won't disturb one another.
- ▪ For brief discussions, three or four persons in one row may stand and face those standing in the row behind.
- ▪ Neighbor-nudging in groups of two works very well even in an auditorium setting.
- ▪ If you plan to do paper work or other activities requiring the use of a table, cut 4′ by 4′ pieces of plywood to place on top of the pew backs.

Because of space shortages, many churches have held classes in buses, outdoor areas (weather permitting), or in nearby homes and commercial buildings.

Most of the Bible learning methods are usable in any kind of situation. A fixed seating arrangement does not affect the usefulness of circle response questions, agree/disagree sheets, tests, questionnaires, evaluation sheets, inductive Bible study methods, research and report projects, and many others. Any activity that can be done well by individuals or in groups of two or three can easily be accomplished in fixed seating arrangements or cramped quarters.

SANCTUARY FIXED SEATING ARRANGEMENTS

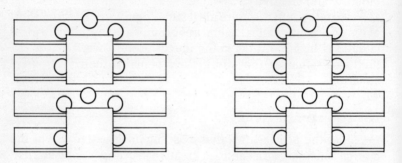

Plywood tables placed over the backs of fixed pews

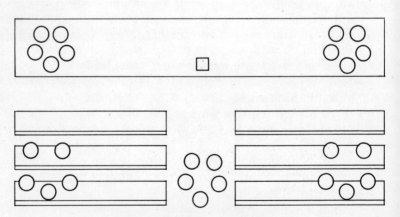

Chairs in the aisles and platform or
small groups in different parts of the sanctuary

WHAT ARE YOU WORKING WITH?

Probably the most important thing to remember is not to let the facilities dictate the type of teaching you do. Rather, use the facilities where they are appropriate, and creatively adapt them when the facilities do not quite fit those described as ideal for the use of certain activities.

Evaluate your adult classroom by using this checklist. For every item you cannot check off, make creative plans to correct the problem.

- ☐ My class is held in an appropriate classroom (rather than the kitchen, or pastor's study)
- ☐ It is located near children's classrooms (if class is for parents)
- ☐ It is on ground floor (if for older adults)
- ☐ It is accessible by wheelchair (if needed)
- ☐ It has enough floor space (10 square feet per adult)
- ☐ The square footage is proportioned correctly
- ☐ There is adequate lighting
- ☐ There is proper ventilation
- ☐ The heating is adequate
- ☐ The cooling system works well
- ☐ Acoustics are good
- ☐ I can darken room for showing films or slides
- ☐ There are electrical outlets for using projectors and other electrical audiovisual equipment
- ☐ It has carpeting
- ☐ There are drapes
- ☐ There are pictures on the wall (or posters)
- ☐ There is storage space for supplies
- ☐ Enough chairs, of proper size, and comfortable
- ☐ A small table
- ☐ Chalkboard and eraser
- ☐ Bulletin board
- ☐ Projection screen

You should keep a supply of these items in the classroom at all times:

- ☐ Chalk
- ☐ Pencils
- ☐ Writing paper
- ☐ Drawing paper
- ☐ Masking tape
- ☐ Felt pens, various colors
- ☐ Scissors
- ☐ Glue
- ☐ Newsprint tablet, or roll of butcher paper
- ☐ 3x5-inch cards

You should keep these resource items in the classroom and have the learners use them as they study God's Word.

- ☐ Extra Bibles, various translations and paraphrases
- ☐ Concordance
- ☐ Bible dictionary
- ☐ English dictionary
- ☐ Bible atlas
- ☐ Bible handbook
- ☐ Set of commentaries
- ☐ Devotional helps

You should have access to and use frequently these items:

- ☐ Overhead projector
- ☐ Opaque projector
- ☐ Slide projector
- ☐ Filmstrip projector
- ☐ Motion picture projector
- ☐ Tape recorder
- ☐ Record player

SOME QUESTIONS TO CONSIDER

1. Why is the environment important in the learning process?
2. List the guidelines for an adult classroom.
3. Diagram a room arranged for small group discussions.
4. Give two ways to use small group discussions in a fixed seating classroom.

The Ministry of Caring

"I'm really hurting inside, but no one in my church knows. We're too busy with the church program to discuss our personal needs."

"Friends at church? I don't have any. There's not enough time on Sundays to develop a friendship."

"We visited that church two or three times but nobody seemed to notice us. It looked like hard work breaking into the 'in-crowd' so we decided not to bother."

Believe it or not, someone has probably made one of those comments about the church you attend. It's sadly true that often Christians are so wrapped up in church work that they neglect the real work of the church—caring for people.

One new way that the spirit of caring is being implemented is through "caring groups." There are many names for caring groups. Some churches call them "circles of concern," others call them "company of the committed" groups or "caring units." By whatever name they are called, these caring groups serve a vital function in the church today. They help to create an atmosphere among twentieth-century believers that is akin to that of the first century, when the believers "devoted themselves to the apostles' teaching and to the fellowship, to the breaking of bread and to prayer" (Acts 2:42, NIV).

WHAT ARE CARING UNITS?

Caring, like anything else that is meaningful in life, seldom just happens. People in a church, just as people in any marriage, tend to drift apart if they don't work at building their relationships to each other. The establishment of caring units is one way of setting up a systematic approach to building meaningful relationships in the church.

A good definition of a caring unit is "People voluntarily meeting together in organized small groups for the purpose of Christian fellowship and edification." There are at least six important reasons for caring units.

1. They provide an opportunity for Christians to know each other and their needs.
2. They help to build relationships between individuals who might ordinarily stay aloof from each other.
3. They encourage the application of the Scripture to life because they permit us to make commitments to each other for "doing the Word."
4. They help meet the social needs which all people have.
5. They promote a sense of belonging for each member.
6. They help Christians fulfill scriptural commands regarding their relationships to one another (see Rom. 12:10,13,15; Gal. 6:2; 1 Thess. 5:11; Heb. 10:24; Jas. 5:16).

HOW ARE CARING UNITS ORGANIZED?

Since the purpose of the caring unit is to build a love relationship within the Body of Christ, they must be as informal and unstructured as possible. Caring units must give each person or group ample opportunity to make choices with respect to relationships and the extent to which he shares himself within that group.

There are three levels on which caring units can be constructed. One is on the basis of *one* independent adult class. In other words, if you are the teacher or director of an adult class and wish to form caring units in your class, there is nothing to prevent you from doing so—and having a successful program.

The second level is to involve *all* the adult classes in a church. Each class may be allowed to make its own choices with respect to how they wish to be grouped and what the functions of their particular caring groups will be. But all the adult Sunday School classes would be involved in the caring unit program.

The third level is one which involves the entire church. There are several ways to organize at this level. One way is to fill each caring unit equally with adult Sunday School attenders and non-attenders. Another way is to organize them by families within the church. Still another way is to encourage people to group themselves voluntarily with just those being involved who wish to be.

There is really no "best" way to organize caring units. However, the existing structure of the adult Sunday School does offer some advantages. The Sunday School is already an organized arm of the church; it is already structured for outreach, fellowship and learning; and the people in the Sunday School are more apt to be motivated to ministry.

The objectives of the caring unit dictate its size. The primary purpose of caring units is to build interpersonal relationships, and meaningful relationships can best be built in small numbers. Therefore we recommend five to six individuals, or five to six couples as an ideal size for a caring unit. When a caring unit grows to nine or ten individuals or couples, plans should be made to divide the group in half to achieve a workable number again.

HOW ARE CARING UNITS FORMED?

Simply stated, caring units must be formed very carefully with ample opportunity for choice being given. Adults resist being put in a box without a choice. Give them at least two alternatives from which to choose in the formation of caring units.

Here are some alternatives which may be offered. Individuals may be *assigned* to a group. The teacher, class leader and perhaps secretary will get together and simply assign everyone to a group from the roll.

Another alternative is for people to *choose* a group to join. In this case you might place sheets of paper on the wall of the class with the name of the caring unit leader at the top. Let the members sign up for the group in which they want to participate. You will need to limit the sign up for each group to the first five or six individuals or couples.

A third alternative is to make a survey of interests or needs and group the people on the basis of the survey results. For example, there might be a group of married couples with children and another group without. They might prefer to be in groups which reflected this difference.

A fourth method is to draw the names out of a hat and form groups at random. People may think of still other possible ways to group themselves. Encourage them to do so but make sure that the objectives for caring units are clear to them.

It is also important to assure people that groups are not permanent. We suggest that you leave them together for at least six months because it takes about that long for good relationships to begin forming. However, they probably should not stay together for more than one year as there is a danger of becoming ingrown and cliquish. Fortunately, the groups grow so fast that it usually is necessary to divide them into new groups within the year.

Show people also that division and occasional reorganization present an opportunity to meet new people, to make new friends. They can have "good-bye" and "welcome" parties. They can keep their old friends while making new ones and really enjoy the fellowship with other Christians. New members who come into the class or church should be added immediately to the existing groups on whatever basis you have chosen.

WHAT HAPPENS IN A CARING UNIT?

What specifically happens in a caring unit will depend a great deal on the needs and schedules of the individuals in it. It should include a combination of biblical input and social enjoyment, both as families and adults only. There are at least six basic formats for caring units.

1. *Bible study for Christian growth.* Small home Bible studies

are one of the amazing success stories in today's churches. These groups not only deepen a Christian's understanding of God's Word but permit him to share its application with his friends so all grow together in spiritual maturity.

2. *Evangelistic Bible study.* The difference between this and number one is essentially one of primary emphasis. In the first case, the emphasis is on Bible study; in the second it is on outreach or evangelism. Both actually should be a part of a home Bible study and caring unit.

3. *Prayer and share.* This format is probably the most common at the present time. The people in the caring unit get together informally to share their joys, sorrows, victories and defeats, and to pray for one another.

4. *Discussion.* These groups may form around the Bible or Christian problems or needs, such as, business ethics, a Christian's participation in politics, etc.

5. *Service projects.* A group may choose to take on caring projects, such as helping a needy family with home repairs or caring for a family where a father is out of work or where there has been a serious illness or accident.

6. *Informal socials.* These can include coffee after church, potluck dinners in the members' homes, game nights, visits to museums, plays, outings in parks, sports events, or hundreds of other social events. Many of these provide an opportunity to involve the families or even prospective members of the class.

Undoubtedly, you and your group can think of other formats for the organization of the caring units. You also could combine some of these formats above as they fit your class.

Caring unit groups should meet as frequently as they feel they can or should, but no less than once a month. Meeting once every two weeks is a plan used by many groups. To build meaningful relationships there has to be a frequency of contact. One group even prays daily by phone with one another.

Most caring units find it best to meet in the homes of the

members. This is more informal, provides a warmer atmosphere, and keeps it away from a "churchy" format, especially beneficial to prospective members who may not be in the church.

WHO WILL LEAD THE CARING UNITS?

Leadership of the caring unit is most important. A good leader can make the program "go"; a bad one or uninterested one may kill the whole project. The following job description from one of the many churches using the caring unit concept may be helpful.

Adult Class Fellowship/Caring Unit Leader Job Description

1. Accepts the leadership of a Fellowship/Caring Unit.
2. Maintains a regular contact with his or her unit members and serves individual unit members and the whole class.
3. Notes the absence in class of his or her unit members and follows up these absentees to let them know they were missed.
4. Provides opportunities to meet together as a unit on a formal or informal basis at least once a month.
5. In cooperation with the class teacher, class leader, pastoral staff, and unit members, determine a format for unit meetings that is acceptable to all involved.
6. Encourages sharing and understanding among his or her unit members.
7. As a class officer, attend class planning meetings.
8. Serve a minimum of six months, with no maximum time limit for those who wish to continue.
9. Invest two hours per week in this ministry.
10. Responsible to the class leader.

Assistance Provided:
1. Resource materials as needed.
2. Training workshops and seminars.
3. Encouragement and assistance from pastoral staff and your class leader.

WHAT ARE THE BENEFITS OF HAVING CARING UNITS?

The main benefit is that caring units encourage better communication and interaction within the structure of the church. Whether a church is large or small, caring groups decrease the change of people's needs going unnoticed. They provide an avenue of communication so that those in teaching roles, whether Sunday School teachers, or a pastor, can have a sense of the pulse of the congregation and of what their needs are, thus enabling them better to minister in the pulpit or the classroom.

And they provide opportunity for new people, whether Christians or not, to be introduced to a group of believers. Where Christ's statement, "By this all men will know that you are My disciples, if you have love for one another" (John 13:35, *NASB*), can be illustrated amid the hectic, impersonal, sometimes grinding pace of modern life.

The potential for benefits in terms of personal friendships and lasting relationships cannot be measured. The potential for personal growth spiritually and socially, as people learn from each other and are challenged by each other, is infinite. Caring groups contribute to the atmosphere of personal maturity.

SOCIALS—ANOTHER WAY TO CARE

"Increasingly, it is in our leisure time that either the meaningfulness or the pointlessness of life will be revealed."[1] Our lives are shaped by our views and involvement in work, community, church, family, and our use of our discretionary time. We all have as much time as the President of the United States. How we choose to use it determines whether or not life is an adventure or a bore, growth or slow death, abundance or poverty of spirit, ministry or suffocating selfishness.

Fellowship, as well as worship, proclamation, witness, teaching, and service is a ministry of the church that contributes to accomplishing its mission. Socials can build fellowship and contribute to wholeness of persons and church growth.

If the purpose of the church and the adult Sunday School class is outreached, then socials are legitimate because they help break down walls between people.

If the ministry of the church includes teaching—helping people learn—socials are productive because they help build relationships that enhance participation and involvement in learning.

If the task of the church is to build the Body of Christ, then socials that open persons to one another and help develop a group feeling are a legitimate concern in "Body life." They help make it possible for members of the Body to communicate with one another at deeper levels of need.

Socials can contribute to meeting the objectives of the adult Sunday School. Outreach, warmth and acceptance, Bible knowledge, and application to life can all be affected positively through socials.

Lyle Schaller, church researcher and planning consultant, says that adult classes with bright futures have several characteristics in common. Here are some that relate to socials.

"The class meets together for some form of social event at least eight or ten times a year. These social events often appear to be the 'glue' that holds the class together. In many classes the Sunday attendance is highest on the Sunday immediately following a monthly social event.

"An important dimension of the social life of the class is when the members eat together several times a year. This may be the monthly social event; it may be an occasional 'covered dish' or 'carry in' dinner; it may be picnics and other outings; it may be only coffee and rolls every Sunday before the class convenes...

"Perhaps most significant of all, the members of these adult classes enjoy being with one another. To some degree every Sunday morning is 'homecoming,' and there is a sense of joy at being together again. Many of the members arrive ten or twenty or thirty minutes early and frequently the class finds it difficult to adjourn on time."[2]

Adults will find some way of using their leisure time; they will socialize somewhere with people or they will sit at home under the spell of the TV. A well-planned social program for your adult Sunday School can turn leisure time into opportunities for caring and outreach, and help bind class members together in the unity of true fellowship. And socials can be just plain fun—and we all need that too!

OTHER WAYS TO CARE

Get to know your adults. One way to be an effective adult teacher is really to know the adults you teach—their joys, sorrows, triumphs, defeats, interests and abilities. The better you know and understand them, the more able you will be to guide them into meaningful Bible study.

How can you get to know the adults you teach? Here are some ways:

1. Invite them over to your house for coffee and dessert, two at a time or in small groups. Chat with them about their families, work, hobbies, interests, etc. Don't try to buttonhole them to join your class. Just let them know you are genuinely interested in them as people. This is a great way to bring in some of the "fringe" people who may be a little shy.

2. Ask several of your class members to help you evaluate your class sessions. Ask them to suggest topics they'd like to discuss, passages of Scripture they'd like to study, changes in teaching procedures they'd like to see incorporated into the class. Every class member should have the opportunity to evaluate the class at regular intervals, but not all are willing to do so verbally. You might distribute paper and pencil some Sunday and ask your learners to write anonymously what they like best about the class, what they like least about the class, topics they'd like to discuss.

3. Duplicate a brief form for your learners to complete and turn in to you. Include space for them to list their name, address,

occupation, amount and kind of education, hobbies and other special interests. You will discover some perhaps unknown talents and interests in your group, talents which can be used in your own class and in other parts of the church program.

4. A variation of number three is to distribute a short form to be completed anonymously with questions asking what they expect from you as a teacher, what they want from the class, are they unsatisfied with their spiritual development, how much responsibility would they be willing to take in order to grow spiritually, and similar questions.

5. Have each class member complete a sentence completion sheet such as the one shown below.

To help me become better acquainted with each member of this class, please complete the following sentences with the *first words* that come to your mind. There are no wrong answers. Do not sign your name.

I wish I were _____
I wish I were not _____
I think God is _____
I think Jesus Christ is _____
I think the Bible is _____
I wish God would _____
The greatest joy of my life is _____
The greatest need of my life is _____
If I could gain just one thing from this class it would be _____

These are just a few suggestions; many others will suggest themselves to you. Brainstorm some ideas for better understanding with your class members.

Provide transportation for disabled persons who wish to attend Sunday School and church services. Some people cannot drive an automobile because of a crippled condition, poor vision, old age, or other disabling causes. A class member can discreetly ask, "Could you attend our Sunday School class or church services if someone picked you up?" Such interest will frequently bear fruit for the cause of Christ.

Choose carefully the people who will provide transportation for the handicapped. They should be patient, discreet and kind. They must be willing to allow additional time to get the person to church before the service begins. Disabled people will likely be slow, cautious and sensitive. Never rush them or allude to their disability. Assure him that he is not a bother or a burden. Try to get the person to church before the other members arrive. His handicap will seem less obvious and he will feel less ill at ease if he is already seated when the others arrive.

Keep in touch with your young people who go away to college or in the service. Put their pictures on the bulletin boards with a brief note about where they are and how long they will be gone. Encourage people to write to these absent members when there is something to share, or just to say "Hi."

If members of your congregation do extensive traveling, urge them to contact these young people from the church in cities where they are visiting or conducting business.

Set aside part of your class time just for sharing what God is doing in the lives of your adults. Introduce this time by asking questions, such as "What's a problem we as a group can join with you in prayer about?" "What's God been doing in your life lately?" "What has God been showing you from His Word in the last few days?"

Sometimes it may seem that your people are not sharing themselves on a very deep level. If you provide time for sharing, however, people will know that there is a place where they will be listened to and cared for. Significant events and crises experiences can be shared with brothers and sisters in Christ.

As you learn about the victories that different individuals have experienced, keep them in mind when you encounter other people facing similar situations. For example, a couple who have overcome marital problems may be willing to share and identify with another couple facing similar difficulties.

Encourage your class members to look for ways to help those who are unable to attend Sunday School and church. Many people, because of sickness or weekend work schedules, are unable to attend church services and thus miss out on needed Bible study and fellowship. An alert adult class can help these people in a variety of ways.

One church circulates books and magazines to shut-ins from the church library. Visitors to the shut-ins take with them a short list of books and magazines available in the library. The shut-in selects the material he would like to read and the visitor sees that the books are delivered to him.

Sometimes the visitor takes Christian literature for the adults to read to children. Grandparents especially were delighted, when they received a wealth of excellent Christian literature to read to their grandchildren. Parents also found literature for their children helpful.

Include shut-ins and others who cannot attend your class regularly on the class roll. Make sure they receive a copy of each quarter's lesson book and weekly church bulletins. Keep them informed of class projects and socials and make them feel welcome whenever they can attend.

Revive some of the neighborly practices of the past! During times of stress, sorrow and deep emotion, it becomes difficult to perform even the routine, familiar functions comfortably. Think back to the last time you felt this way, and seek to understand and meet the needs of your Christian friends when they are having these problems. Illness, death in the family, birth of a new baby, a personal disaster (fire, flood) are obvious times of need; conflict on the job, within the family, periods of depression, loneliness are not always recognized as periods of need also.

How can you care? Think of the routine things that might be just added, unbearable problems at this time. For example: washing the car, cooking, driving the children to baseball practice, picking up the dry cleaning, mowing the lawn, caring for small children 24-hours a day, even grocery shopping. Which of these things could you do for them? Granted that you already have these things to do for your own family, and granted that you might normally do these things for a close friend, this is an opportunity for you to share God's love. And God's love is not just spoken words, it is outward actions.

A MODEL OF CARING

To borrow an often used rhyme, caring is caught, easier than taught. If your class is to become a group of deeply caring persons they must have a model to "infect" them with a caring heart. You can be that model. Your personal ministry of caring to your class will result in them becoming caring individuals themselves.

SOME QUESTIONS TO CONSIDER

1. How are people being cared for in your Sunday School class?

2. Do you have caring units (or a reasonable facsimile) established for the adults of your church? If so, how have they contributed to the ministry of caring in your church? If not, what steps do you need to take in order to form caring units?

3. How can socials build the ministry of caring among class members? How can socials complement your class outreach?

4. In what ways can you improve as a caring model? When will you start?

FOOTNOTES

1. Robert Lee, *Religion and Leisure in America* (Nashville: Abingdon, 1964), p. 26.
2. Lyle Schaller, *Hey, That's Our Church!* (Nashville: Abingdon, 1975), pp. 145-147.

Evaluating Your Teaching Ministry

The leaders who carefully set objectives for their Sunday School, develop plans to meet those objectives, and implement those plans have taken the first steps toward successfully ministering to their adults.

But you can't stop there! For the best laid plans can be roadblocked by the many unexpected problems which arise. Therefore, a wise leader evaluates his Sunday School frequently to see if it is progressing as planned.

There are at least four specific reasons to evaluate your Sunday School. Ask yourself these questions:

1. *Is it functioning effectively?* Are you meeting the objectives you set for your Sunday School? Are your adults experiencing warmth and acceptance? Are they studying the Word and applying it to their lives? Are they reaching other adults for Christ? If so, terrific! If not, you'll want to determine what is blocking those objectives.

2. *Is it functioning efficiently?* Are there any ways to simplify or improve procedures or processes on the Sunday School while still maintaining effectiveness?

3. *Are there problems?* New and unexpected problems are a

fact of life! Your Sunday School will have its share. So, you will want to have a method of discovering and solving problems as they arise. Remember that the problem areas will vary from week to week or month to month. Be aware of your priorities, so that your problem-solving attention is focused on the area of greatest need at any given time.

4. *Are there new needs?* When you discover new areas of needs in your adult Sunday School, be responsive—set new goals. These may be short-term plans to meet short-term needs, or even major plans to serve long-term needs.

WHAT TO EVALUATE

Evaluation should be extended to every part of the Sunday School class and every level of responsibility. In fact, the success of the evaluation will be determined by how specific the evaluation is. If you ask yourself, "Are we teaching the learners?" you will probably get an affirmative answer. But what part of the teaching is effective and what parts could be improved? How else will you know, unless you evaluate the specifics of the program? Therefore, you should evaluate the following kinds of details:

1. *The facilities:* equipment, room design, which classes are assigned to which classrooms, lighting, temperature, need for painting or repairs.

2. *The communications:* laterally—between the various staff members; upwards—from learners to teachers, teachers to department leaders and others; and downwards—from the general superintendent to the department leaders and on down to the teachers and others.

3. *The staffing ratios:* Are the classes the best size? Are the department leaders supervising from one to five teachers? Are the divisional coordinators over one to five department leaders?

4. *The leaders:* Are the leaders satisfied with their "assignments"? Do some want to rotate and work with another class?

Are there problems which need to be discussed? What about the working relationships?

5. *The sessions:* Are there problems? Should the session be lengthened, the order of the blocks of time be switched, the responsibilities changed?

6. *The curriculum:* Is the current curriculum still meeting the need? Are the illustrations appropriate? Is the content at the proper level for the learners?

7. *The planning meetings:* Are they frequent enough, conducted correctly, covering the right material, a waste of time? Do enough leaders attend? Should the date be changed?

8. *The training:* Is more needed than is being provided? Is a different type of training needed? Who should conduct the training? Which type of training seems to be the most effective?

9. *The attendance:* Which classes show a high rate of absenteeism? Why? What percent of the enrollment of the entire Sunday School is in regular attendance? How can the percentage be increased? How can the enrollment be increased?

10. *The interest:* Do the learners seem interested in the classes? Which methods do they like best? Which methods do they seem to learn the most from? How is the interest shown?

11. *The Sunday School objectives:* What things should the Sunday School accomplish? How? When? In what way and to what degree? Do you want to continue with the same basic objectives or do you feel you should change the emphasis of the Sunday School in your own church?

These items are only suggestions. Only you can decide what to evaluate in your own Sunday School. You must also select the best method and time for evaluation.

HOW TO EVALUATE

You must decide which evaluative device will be most useful in determining the effectiveness and efficiency of your own Sunday School. Here are three effective methods:

1. Check the statistics.
2. Solicit feedback from the staff and the learners.
3. Set specific, measurable, short-term goals.

Check the Statistics

Your Sunday School records are filled with valuable statistics which will help you evaluate.

What is the total enrollment? What percentage of that enrollment is in regular attendance? Which classes show the highest percentage in attendance? Which show the lowest rate in attendance? What is the census of the neighborhood around the church? What percent of the available population in the area attend your Sunday School?

What has been the rate of growth of your Sunday School over the last year? Which classes have grown the fastest? Which have not grown? What effect has starting new classes had on the growth rate?

How much and what type of personal contact have the Sunday School leaders made over the last three months? How many personal visits? How many telephone calls? How many postcards were sent out? Did the attendance increase in those classes with the most personal contacts?

Analyze these statistics and present your conclusions and recommendations to the Sunday School staff.

Solicit Feedback from the Staff and the Learners

You will get a good idea of the attitude and feelings of the people in your Sunday School if you encourage feedback from them. You need not be tied down by the complaints and suggestions made by the learners and the staff. But listen attentively to the opinions expressed and be guided by them whenever possible.

You can get feedback from a suggestion box (no complaints please, without a suggestion for a solution!!!); a questionnaire checklist; or an opinionnaire with "stub end questions" for the staff and/or the entire Sunday School to complete.

Informal feedback should be encouraged in staff meetings, planning meetings and at any time during the week.

Set Specific, Measurable, Short-term Goals

Once a need is determined, the group of leaders involved should work as a group and set up a plan of action. Each step would be specific, measurable and have a due date. A time to evaluate the plan and the action should be set and followed through. You might use a project board for those projects which will take a period of one quarter or more. This will be a visual reminder of the project and a reassurance of the progress being made. At any one time, you will know exactly where you are going, where you are now and what is left to do.

Once this process is organized and operational, it is the easiest and most efficient way to accomplish the objectives of the Sunday School.

WHEN TO EVALUATE

If a problem arises, you will of course evaluate the cause and possible solutions right then. But the major items in the Sunday School program also need periodic evaluation.

For example, you might evaluate the space assignments, curriculum and leaders once a year—probably a few months before promotion and the new "year" starts. For most churches, the new year starts in September, concurrent with the beginning of the secular school year. Plan the evaluation for the summer so that you allow enough time to initiate changes as a result of the evaluation.

Short-term goals should be set on a quarterly basis for most projects. Therefore, you should evaluate them every quarter and set new goals or extend the time on the current ones.

Evaluating is like mowing the lawn. If you keep it up, it isn't too much of a problem, but if you let it go, the task becomes monumental!

SOME QUESTIONS TO CONSIDER

1. Write four reasons why you should evaluate your Sunday School.

2. Describe the elements of the Sunday School which can be evaluated.

3. Give three evaluative techniques you might use in your Sunday School.

4. What about your Sunday School? When was the last time your staff evaluated their program? What did they evaluate? How? What areas did they forget to evaluate?

5. When did you last evaluate your area of responsibility in the Sunday School? What methods did you use? What plans for change did you make after that evaluation? Did your plans result in needed changes?

6. Evaluate an area of your responsibility for efficiency and effectiveness. Set three quarterly goals to improve your efforts in that area. List the specific steps you will take to reach your goals within a set period of time. Plan when and how you will evaluate your progress. Begin working on your plan. Stick to it! Follow through!

Bibliography

Bergevin, Paul; Morris, Dwight and Smith, Robert M. *Adult Education Procedures*. New York: Seabury Press, 1963.

Burnham, David and Sue. *A Bible Study in My House?* Chicago: Moody Press, 1975.

Edge, Findley. *Helping the Teacher*. Nashville: Broadman Press, 1959.

Edge, Findley, *Teaching for Results*. Nashville: Broadman Press, 1956.

Edge, Findley. *The Greening of the Church*. Waco: Word Publishers, 1971.

Ezell, Mansell and Suzanne. *Being Creative*. Nashville: Broadman Press, n.d.

Ford, LeRoy. *Primer for Teachers and Leaders*. Nashville: Broadman Press, 1963.

Ford, LeRoy. *Tools for Teaching and Training*. Nashville: Broadman Press, 1961.

Ford, LeRoy. *Using the Case Study in Teaching and Training*. Nashville: Broadman Press, 1970.

Ford, LeRoy. *Using the Lecture in Teaching and Training*. Nashville: Broadman Press, 1968.

Ford, LeRoy. *Using the Panel in Teaching and Training*. Nashville: Broadman Press, 1971.

Flynn, Elizabeth W. and La Faso, John F. *Group Discussion as Learning Process: A Sourcebook*. New York: Paulist Press, 1972.

Garvin, Marry. *Bible Study Can Be Exciting!* Grand Rapids: Zondervan, 1976.

Gehris, Paul D. *Using the Bible in Group*. Valley Forge: Judson Press, 1973.

Getz, Gene A. *Sharpening the Focus of the Church.* Chicago: Moody, 1974.

Getz, Gene A. *The Measure of a Church.* Glendale, CA: Regal Books, 1975.

Holt, D. Allison. *Learning About Methods.* St. Louis: Christian Board of Publication.

Howard, Walden. *Groups that Work.* Grand Rapids: Zondervan, 1967.

Hunt, Gladys. *It's Alive.* Wheaton, IL: Harold Shaw Publishers, 1971.

Joy, Donald M. *Meaningful Learning in the Church.* Winona Lake, IN: Light and Life Press, 1969.

Kemp, Charles F. *Prayer-Based Growth Groups.* Nashville: Abingdon Press, 1974.

Klevins, Chester (ed.). *Materials and Methods in Adult Education.* New York: Klevens Publications Inc., 1972.

Knowles, Malcolm. *The Adult Learner: A Neglected Species.* Houston: Gulf Publishing Company, 1973.

Knowles, Malcolm. *The Modern Practice of Adult Education.* New York: Association Press, 1970.

Kunz, Marilyn and Schell, Catherine. *How to Start a Neighborhood Bible Study.* Wheaton, IL: Tyndale House Publishers, 1966.

Leslie, Robert C. *Sharing Groups in the Church.* Nashville: Abingdon Press, 1970.

Leypoldt, Martha M. *40 Ways to Teach in Groups.* Valley Forge, PA: Judson Press, 1971.

Leypoldt, Martha M. *Learning Is Change.* Valley Forge, PA: Judson Press, 1971.

Little, Lawrence C. *Wider Horizons in Christian Adult Education.* Pittsburgh, PA: University of Pittsburgh Press, 1962.

Lum, Ada. *How to Begin an Evangelistic Bible Study.* Downers Grove, IL: InterVarsity Press, 1971.

Mager, Robert F. *Developing Attitude Toward Learning.* Belmont, CA: Fearon Publishers, 1968.

Mager, Robert F. *Preparing Instructional Objectives*. Belmont, CA: Fearon Publishers, 1962.

Minor, Harold. *Creative Procedures for Adult Groups*. Nashville: Abingdon Press, 1968.

Minor, Harold (ed.). *Techniques and Resources for Guiding Adult Groups*. Nashville: Abingdon Press, 1972.

Morrison, Eleanor S. and Foster, Virgil E. *Creative Teaching in the Church*. Englewood Cliffs, N.J.: Prentice-Hall, 1963.

Pierce, Rice. *Leading Dynamic Bible Study*. Nashville: Broadman Press, 1969.

Raths, Louis E.; Harmin, Merrill; Simon, Sidney B. *Values and Teaching*. Columbus, OH: Charles E. Merrill Publishing Co., 1966.

Reed, Marlowe, and Collins. *Sunday School Teachers Planbook: Adult*. Glendale, CA: G/L Publications, 1975.

Richards, Lawrence O. *Creative Bible Study*. Grand Rapids: Zondervan, 1971.

Richards, Lawrence O. *You—the Teacher*. Chicago: Moody Press, 1972.

Richards, Lawrence O. *Creative Bible Teaching*. Chicago: Moody Press, 1970.

Richards, Lawrence O. *A Theology of Christian Education*. Grand Rapids: Zondervan, 1975.

Richards, Lawrence O. *69 Ways to Start a Study Group and Keep It Growing*. Grand Rapids: Zondervan, 1973.

Roper, David. *Teacher with a Visual Punch*. Cincinnati: Standard Publishing, n.d.

Schacher, James A. *Conversational Bible Studies*. Grand Rapids: Baker Book House, 1975.

Schaller, Lyle E. *Hey, That's Our Church!* Nashville: Abingdon, 1975.

Sheehy, Gail. *Passages: Predictable Crises of Adult Life*. New York: E. P. Dutton and Co., Inc., 1974.

Simon, Howe and Kirschenbaum. *Values Clarification*. New York: Hart Publishing Company, Inc., 1972.

Walk, Oletta. *The Joy of Teaching Discovery Bible Study.* Minneapolis: Augsburg Publishing House, 1976.

Williams, James D. *Guiding Adults.* Nashville: Convention Press, 1969.

Wollen, Albert J. *How to Conduct Home Bible Classes.* Wheaton, IL: Scripture Press Publications, 1969.

Wollen, Albert J. *Miracles Happen In Group Bible Study.* Glendale, CA: G/L Publications, 1976.

Zuck, Roy B. and Getz, Gene A. *Adult Education in the Church.* Chicago: Moody Press, 1970.